I0104105

THE
SOCIAL RESEARCH
FOUNDATION
DOCUMENTARY
PRINT

by Carol Sill

ISBN 0-9781705-1-2
Copyright © Carol Sill, 2006, all rights reserved
Cover by Carol Sill

Alpha Glyph Publications Ltd.
16 East Cordova Street, #B
Vancouver BC V6A 1K2

Documentary Print
by Carol Sill

FOREWORD

These documents are a synthesis of my experience and study of communications, art and society. They were written over a period of two years, mostly in Banff in the Canadian Rockies. They form a sort of bureaucratic story and are intended as a philosophical art piece. The Interim Report on Living in the Future was circulated by mail in 1983 as an art document, including the questionnaire which received many replies. Other sections have been performed in readings.

Carol Sill, Vancouver, 2006

Why Present This Material?
The answer is obvious: Public Information.
The Social Research Foundation firmly believes that the public must have access to all information.
This Documentary Print is the public disclosure of such information.

Public release of documents such as these reveals to the general public the be-hind-the-scenes research work which is now shaping them demo/psychographi-cally. The status quo is maintained by consistent shared public dreams kept in a balanced equation. Information disclosure can give the dream equation a possibility of shifting, which allows a capacity for evolution in society at large.
In the SRF, document release is usually carefully monitored. In this case, however, the situation seriously requires a full disclosure of all written materials.
Yet much of the material is not marketable, so the Research Context Committee and the Edit/Format Group are handling the controlled release of appropriate information only.
The other, non-marketable materials will remain available, on view at SRF HQ for 10 years (appt. by request) after which time the information contained in the documents will have been publicly absorbed and considered as Common Knowledge.

THE CONTEXT

After much deliberation, the Research Context Committee (RCC) has agreed to present these documents in a frame of Social Science Fiction.

Possible approaches, listed below, were basically broken down into five separate areas:

1. The Factual Report
2. New Journalism
3. Incendiary Internal Documents
4. Social Science Fiction
5. Choose Your Own Context

The fifth, a multiple choice, was deemed the most accurate, but was eventually rejected by the committee as being too complex for the average reader, and therefore detracting from the text itself. See Alternate Presentation Modes, Appendix II for a fuller explanation.

To introduce these documents to the general public, many minds deliberated carefully as to the most appealing presentation frame. Market surveys and demo/psychographic testing indicated that this material was not of interest to most people at first glance. However, independent research has shown that IN THE FUTURE, this type of idea-presentation would become Common Knowledge. Therefore, the SOCIAL SCIENCE FICTION frame was considered most appropriate, appealing as it does to the forward-thinking. (By "appropriate" is meant "marketable").

Market considerations also influence the Edit/Format Group which has lifted out many sections from the available documentation, and which has therefore prepared the presented material in a biased form for marketing purposes only. Such cosmetic manipulation enhances the availability of the ideas here presented, without seriously detracting from the total intent of the work itself. It is the reader's insight and discretion which will discern fact from "enhanced fact" (i.e. fiction) in this material. Illustrations have also been included to break the monotony of the print medium (not available in this version.)

A debt of gratitude is owed to the first presenter of this material to the committee and to the many unsung researchers and reporters working continuously in the field of SOCIAL RESEARCH.

IMPORTANT INSERT:
Shaman Poem Fragment

RIDE THEM. THEY GO. THEY GO UP.
THEY GO UP THE STARS.
THE STARS.
HEY BIG ONE!
RIDE THEM, THEY GO UP.

Social Science Fiction (SSF)   INTRODUCTION

THE
SOCIAL RESEARCH
FOUNDATION

DOCUMENTARY PRINT

THE LABORER FILE

Introduction

IN THE EARLY 1980'S
    This volume provides a window into a world gone by. In the early 1980's, an organization sprang up, using the title SOCIAL RESEARCH FOUNDATION or SRF. With banks of researchers, reporters and contacts worldwide, the SRF appears to have analyzed social trends on an unprecedented scale. Today, such an approach is not unusual, but then it was extremely rare.

THE DOCUMENTS WERE FOUND
    When the documents were found, they had been abandoned in the home of a laborer. Despite their obvious antiquity, he did nothing to notify museum authorities concerning them and it was only after his death that the SRF DOCUMENTARY PRINT was discovered and translated.

KEPT IN METAL BOXES
    The information discovered on site (Laborer File) are in fact parts of larger document files which had been distributed worldwide. Much of the greater file was siezed during the Reconstruction, and subsequently lost. The Laborer File is in excellent condition, and appears to have been kept in metal boxes which preserved most of the documents, although heat fused all other data.

GENUINE SOCIAL RESEARCH
    Analogous material has been retrieved in northern areas which were not affected as deeply. Therefore it is possible to correlate data and authenticate this material as genuine SOCIAL RESEARCH DATA.

A RENEGADE RESEARCH NODE

Interestingly, much of the information found in this file cannot be correlated within the general SRF data collection as it is to date. Indicators point to a "renegade" research node, involved perhaps in research unsanctioned by headquarters. The SRF appears to have been a highly centralized operation, with a comprehensive total training program and little evidence of dissent. If this new Laborer File indicates dissent, and it does seem to document internal confusion in the research organization, then a definite historical breakthrough occurs with the release of this document.

THE OFFICIAL TRANSLATION

What follows is the official translation of all found SRF documents in the Laborer File. Roughly arranged in chronological order, they refer to the time period 1983-85. After that point, the reports appear to have all been done in visual or ritual form. There is unfortunately no record of these later reports.

THOSE WERE DARKER TIMES

History is always fascinating. To us, looking back, it appears the SRF was extremely far-seeing in its understanding of events and analyses which we now take for granted. Those were darker times, and few, if any, could perceive the seeds of our present society.

TABLE OF CONTENTS

THE LABORER FILE
Table of Contents

1
A RESEARCHER'S DIARY

Contents
1. Fragment from the Researcher Manual
2. The Diary

Translator's note: This diary fragment was found with the documents of the Laborer File. It gives an unusual record of the thoughts and feelings of a common researcher, as well as giving insight into the workings of the SRF on a day to day basis. With it has also been found a partial page of the Researcher Manual, which had been kept presumably by the diarist, at the beginning of the diary.

1. Fragment from the Researcher Manual

It can be seen that research is the only worthwhile aspect of present life. Although to a beginner reported research seems unrelated to daily life, it will show itself in time to be clearly prototypical.

Those who lack emotional clarity, a needed attribute of researchers generally, cannot handle the waves of reality manifested through this research. When a researcher's life becomes more linked to this form of understanding, freedom from emotional upheaval becomes easier to achieve. Remember: Feelings and experiences do not constitute "reality" in essence.

Entering all experience as a Social Researcher offers immense freedom even in the constrictions of everyday life. This gives the detachment of "observation by involvement" which is a keynote of the approach now favored by the SRF.

Future analysis will yield many observations to be proven at later . . . .

2. The Diary

DIARY DAY 1

With all the stress of research, I felt it might be helpful to develop this diary. Without the information encoding used now in rapid report phases, this simple "early writing form" will help me sort out my own responses to the data I now collect and analyze.

It is all very well to be used continually by the Foundation as a prime researcher, and truly, I am grateful, but if I am ever to understand just what it is I am researching, and just what it is I am reporting, then this diary may be my first step.

I wonder if I should tell others at the Foundation about this step? I'll just let it sit for a while. Somehow, I feel it might upset them. Going along on my own, I mean, reporting to myself rather than to the whole foundation. But should that be subversive? I do a good job - one of the best if I do say so, and I am entitled to free time to use as I please.

Most of the other researchers tend to stick together after hours. When you are so highly specialized, especially in research areas, it is practically impossible to have a real conversation with anyone outside the field. Contact with lay people immediately becomes another chance for research, and you end up without any relief.

For me, to spend all my time at the usual hangouts doesn't work anymore. There is something missing and I just can't pinpoint it yet. Maybe there are others who feel that way too - what if there are others keeping diaries!? I'm going to keep my eyes open for signs - they won't tell me outright, after all I am a prime researcher and many aren't as experienced as I am. Some of my trainees are now full reporters and one or two have become #1A. They see me as their superior, and would never expose personal attributes which aren't part of our PERSONALIZED CHARACTERIZATION OF PERSONA PACKAGE. They probably don't even have them! The personal attributes, I mean. At least they won't have them if I did my job right. But that's going a bit far. We decided in the Report Document on Living in the Future that privacy was to be found in all that cannot be encoded. Why should I have my quirks and idiosyncrasies while the young zealots are smooth and quirk-free? It comes from me being a founder, and them being followers who believe in the packaging. I suppose they will grow.

The Foundation does have more than a few cracks these days. Although I was one of the founders, I was young then, and secondary to the process as it was evolving. Not that I am that old now, but research, active and unrelenting, pushed me into the future so I feel old, seem old to myself. I must find a way to recover that youth. Do I really want it now, knowing what I now know about the tendencies today?

Just returning to this language makes me feel younger, for it is only used for the expressing of immature thoughts, for emotional nuances, for feelings.

I have so needed to express these ideas somehow, any way at all! This diary is the perfect way. Perhaps sometime it will be discovered and read not just by me, but by others. Isn't this the secret dreaded wish of every diarist?

I only know that without this diary, my research would suffer terribly. And I don't want that. I am so dedicated to the field and the principles that it is practically obsessive. I have such a drive to do well, I mean Really Well, that the tension knots me inside until sleep is impossible for 3 or 4 nights at a time. Needless to say, my research suffers greatly when that goes on. What I love about this diary is that I don't have to think about the Foundation, I don't have to do well, and I don't have to analyze my reactions with attractive packaging. This language is naive, it is mine - a simple conversational form I learned years ago among friends and family.

They did have some trouble with me a while back so they may be watching for something to shift. I've seen them go over and over my reports, looking for signs of the old instability but they will never find them. My work today is flawless. I can apply and replace PATTERN GUARD with ease, and my training is always to the fore. I can be cool, as they said in the past. And my certain fluency gives me the courage to try, to dig out this old fashioned notebook, which is a mirror of thought, to begin the diary. I am excited to see what comes next.

I have to add, or is it admit, that it was love, or what I thought was love, that caused the trouble. I suppose it couldn't be avoided and doesn't everyone go through it? Sometime I must write about it in here. I haven't been quite right since. My PATTERN GUARD is fine, but at night ....well, I already went over that. Until tomorrow....

I couldn't wait! (Oh Pattern Guard where are you now?) I have to say that I am collecting some reports, not many, which I am keeping only to myself. If it is appropriate I may put them into this diary. Once I'm sure it is safe. Even writing this down is stupid actually, but I learned in training that reporting is the only cure. These reports I have aren't strange - they just don't fit SRF criteria, and I find them interesting.

There has never been a known case of freelancing on the side before, so it may all be above board. I'd like to see all reporters active on all fronts. But I just have the feeling that I should sit on these for the time being and just observe. The timing is essential. Meanwhile, I'll report them here in the diary when it seems right. There. I did it. And it wasn't hard at all! I admitted to myself, my mirror, what I have done. Oh, I suddenly wonder, do other researchers feel the same? Have they all done it and I am the last to know? They are all so well-trained, its impossible to imagine. As far as I know, I'm the only one who had to go through full retraining. The SRF will never let anyone go, either. The field is just too new actually for anyone to know just what the ground rules are. Oh, we pretend all right, managing to convince would-be reporters that the whole thing is tight and understandable and neatly arranged. I wonder, are senior researchers and founders just as confused, or more?

Wouldn't this be a great joke? My discovery that it is really just a free-for-all was in fact a promotion to full researcher category, to the ranks of the few old-time founders? I'm going to probe this situation. My research instincts are all alert and I could be on to something here.

DIARY DAY 2

Today is my day off. I'll have time to write some of the past events - no rush or deadlines. I didn't go out with the gang, so I'm just home - even prime researchers have to do the laundry!

When I woke up this morning I toyed with the idea of having two diaries - one for this sort of thing and another for - what? Probably for the impressions and writings I would never want discovered by anyone else. A raw diary. Deeper. But there may not be a need for it - this may be as deep as it gets!

Last night I slept so soundly and without dreams. I feel completely rested and calm. My sentences here are short and simple. Mind at ease for the first time in months. Then come a series of images from the future: my diary has been confiscated. They intend to use it as an example. But of what? I see myself reading the diary of another researcher. It practically shocks me. It makes so little sense. I wonder if the other researcher is me, if the diary I read is my own, progressed beyond recognition.

Ever since I began active work on the future, images have entered my mind, standing before me. Until now, I took no notice of them, as we were instructed in training. Often they have nothing to do with future patterns at all, but only seem to be from the future at the time of vieiwng. I'm not making sense at all.

Tomorrow.

DIARY DAY 3

Before work.

Many of the ideas which were swirling for prominence have been tamed by these few diary entries. I was calm and ordered - collected they say - until I put pen to paper again. Something about opening this little book, willing that mirror into existence - it is as if I were splitting open as the pages open. Logic seems to fly out the window and I am left raving on paper. Raving, raving, about what? The articulation is still unclear, because frankly I am afraid to enter into that world clearly.

I was thinking yesterday of this diary as a fantasy world. I seem to be writing about my life, about discovery - it is very soothing and relaxing after a week of research. The fantasy could be that the diary helps.

It doesn't help. It just perpetuates a parallel world and is setting me up for some drastic conflict. By consciously closing out the research mode (which is, after all, my life) and instead writing into existence the simple pre-research person I was as a child, I could be in dangerous territory. Not only that, this person of the diary doesn't actually exist. The one who is the active researcher, the well-chosen persona, is far more real than this small worded voice here in the diary. So I didn't continue writing yesterday, as I had intended. It seemed a waste of time.

Why do I feel this conflict? It should be quite straightforward - if I am writing the diary then that is what I am doing, if not then I carry on as before. What is the confusion? It is that as I work on the diary I change. Yes I am calmer, that is true. But there is an undercurrent of confusion, upheaval. I guess I am afraid of uncontrolled feelings, and of these feelings seeping into my work life, of research that is useless to the Foundation and of love. I have been perfectly retrained, why chip at the retraining now, after so long?

****

It was a hectic day and I just had to add this before going to bed. I talked to a friend today - a former researcher who had dropped out for a sabbatical. What I mean to say here is that I told him - it just blurted out (my god, where is that pattern guard?) I told him about the diary. But I didn't say it was mine - I just said I was writing something in the form of a diary, the innermost thoughts and feelings of this person. He immediately said, "So you've discovered the novel." Now if I had been clever and in training mind, I would have agreed and it would be fine. But the Guard was completely shifted off, and I said, "Well, no, it's not really like that. It's real..." and on and on. But it never actually opened, thank heavens, despite my obvious stupidity. It doesn't really matter because he wouldn't tell, nor be interested actually. I don't know why I told him and can't say why I responded so unthinkingly. I must watch more carefully over these reactions - they could become difficult for me.

DIARY DAY 4

Too busy yesterday to take a minute for the diary. Today shapes up the same. I'm into a fascinating research area which is also very enjoyable to me so I don't miss the diary. Just to keep continuity I carry on here today. I won't write about the research as that will be for SRF reports - I don't know what form they'll choose for these ones - could be anything at all at this stage. Must go to prepare for the day...

***

Evening! How could I have been so wrong? I needed this diary more today than ever, and if I could have written in it this afternoon it may have saved a lot of trouble. Getting into an argument with another researcher (on the nature of research of all things, something we know to be entirely subjective) was not what I had in mind for today's work. It began this morning with a really mild conversation which was escalated by both of us into something out of proportion. I guess I'm not the only one under research-stress these days. And when it was over, I just felt so terrible, energyless and bleak. We were good colleagues, so I feel confident that we will be able to work together again. And this afternoon it was impossible to keep my fresh mind. Instead, I just went over and over that conversation.

If I'd had my diary with me, I could have noted it and carried on. As it was, the day was a washout - most unfortunate for the SRF and for everyone concerned. I really hope they don't notice my lapse. Then I had to see the Foundation physician about my blackout spells. I intend to spend the evening in a relaxed mode.

I won't seek lowlevel stimulus though, because in this frame I prefer any upliftment which would lead me to fresh mind again. It is so true what we learned in training: reporting is the only relief. What I never imagined was that I would use the training advice in my personal life. But that's because when I was in training I didn't have a personal life. Research was all.

We were led to believe we were all to become PERFECTLY TYPICAL - to homogenize into one family with all of us having the same attributes, the same viewpoint, the same attitudes. How different it all became once we were actually in the field. The training team isn't to blame. They were only hypothesising. We knew from the beginning how experimental it all was. That was what attracted some of us most.

But I feel betrayed somehow when I see how the best minds of the time were recruited and seduced into the research field like old-time soldiers and seacrew - just taken before you could think. And no one was prepared for the intense loneliness of research and discovery. The SRF founders felt that they could experimentally attempt a group formation. To some extent it has really worked, but the problem of individuality just never was resolved. The only real research occurs when the researcher is alone exploring unknown territory. And reporting back - well, it's all in the DOCUMENT ON LIVING IN THE FUTURE, why repeat?

Right now, all prime researchers are in a LINK-LAUNCH of approximately the same velocity and intensity, each in a different direction. It's another experiment on simultaneous research in varied fields - linked only by research itself. Why such an effort should cause conflict or confrontation, I just don't understand. We give up "attachment to personal view" in the first course of training.

DIARY DAY 5

There are problems with the LINK-LAUNCH. I haven't had a moment to catch up here in the diary because of them. Most researchers weren't ready for it when it began, and some entirely misunderstood their instructions. This has led to some very strange circumstances. I can't describe it all now..... there is so little diary time these days. I just flop into bed at the end of the day and get up to begin work. Funny feeling -- it's as if I've lost myself when I can't write in the diary.

DIARY DAY 6

An older research consultant called late last night with an odd request: she wants me to scan data she sent to me one year ago. This data was personal, relating to me, using an anachronistic divining science popular with the Anti-Techs. Forecasting a disastrous year for me. I wasn't about to scan it then, knowing what I do about impressions creating experience, but maybe now I can. And with the help of the diary to decode it all, I could have a new perspective on it. I never have understood this woman, who is otherwise a brilliant social scientist. Why does she stoop to these weird illogical thought constructs? Some days she refuses to work if the signs are inauspicious. Needless to say, no one could run a research organization based on such principles.

Not that I am not attracted to the Anti-Tech stance. Some of their approaches to life strangely correspond to the SRF future findings.

Now that I have a moment, I'll get into the LINK-LAUNCH. It isn't working at this stage because, although intensity and velocity were equal in starting, many researchers have resistance which slows both intensity and velocity after launch. The manifestation of this resistance (either in the lives of reseachers or in their work approach) has made some of us enemies, others untrusting, others confused, and a few are dropping out. Simultaneously, four went on leaves of absence. Yet the LINK-LAUNCH is being continued by the SRF despite these findings. I can't understand what they are trying to achieve. I myself am so exhausted by it that I can barely drag myself out of bed most mornings.

DIARY DAY 7

I think LINK-LAUNCH is almost over! There has been a gap - the pressure has lessened so I feel more hopeful of success now. As I integrate to prepare report data, I find myself grateful for the LINK-LAUNCH. I just hope everyone else feels the same or we will have a dreadful split in the Foundation.

DIARY DAY 8

I wish I could record everything in the diary but the pressure of my work really only alows these few notes. My hopes for the diary just haven't materialized it seems. Work and research outside work-hours have really dominated my waking hours. But I do think of the diary from time to time throughout the day. The SRF will elaborate on LINK-LAUNCH when results are in. I now must study the works of parallel researchers in order to context new non-linear data. I love this aspect of the work. I haven't faltered at all lately, nor have I felt the need to talk about the diary anymore.

Having recently changed research areas, I am now eager to begin my new work and am definitely frustrated with finishing off the old work load.

Lately I have had thoughts of my uncle, whom I haven't seen since I began this primary work. It was in his books that I began to glimpse the beginnings of social research, and I wonder now if he was one of the proto-researchers mentioned in training. Conversations with him were pivotal to my whole life. When he sent me the address of the primary research founder of the SRF, I really wasn't surprised, but it took me 6 months to make the call.

Sometime I'll go into the training school experience. For now comes much needed sleep. Not that sleep revives the missing elan vital. I find myself wondering if my uncle ever used to feel this way, sitting in his chair late at night.

DIARY DAY 9

Yesterday I met an interesting man who never uses his CHARACTERIZATION OF PERSONA PACKAGE (CPP). He is some kind of artist and seems to want to be recognized in the merit of his art. Of course, without using the CPP he gets nowhere and therefore his work is virtually unknown. I told him of the value of CPP use for everyday events, something we researchers study early on in training. This made me think about how we researchers manipulate the CPP to advantage - putting forward one which is useful for the research at hand, cutting off one which we may have seemed to identify with.

I said that artists could use the research attitude to handle CPP and then there would be no integrity problem. At least, I don't think so, but he felt differently. He was trying to live in the recent past by not allowing the erasure of Personal Identity (PI), which has been such a useful change for researchers. Now I know that this diary is a recovery of PI but basically I operate as instructed from chosen CPP with PI erased. It has only been since the diary began that I have felt PI again and it is very excruciating, and old-fashioned, like guilt or shame or embarrassment. Too exposed without shelter. How can anyone have lived continuously in such a mode? It seems impossible to me now.

So this artist was an anachronistic relic, living an outmoded self-view so completely. He tries to blend in, but of course it is obvious from his facial gestures that he is not actually participating. It's funny, isn't it, that I have the feeling that if I hadn't begun this diary, he and I might never have met.

Must go to work. The assignment I thought had been completed is now reactivated. It was an old exploration of past known data, which didn't interest me then and is even less attractive now. That's another thing about this artist. His PI wasn't attractive either. He acted as if he knew me. That would have been disturbing to me weeks ago, but now I have too much work to do to be bothered.

DIARY DAY 10

One week since the last entry. An intense research field test has monopolized all time. Great impasses followed by stunning breakthroughs, like a mountain storm.

It has been one of the most satisfying and involving research bursts. So strong, in fact, that I really have nothing to write in the diary. The onrush of experience through research has been so vivid, vital and genuine that the little persona of the diary cannot word or even conceive of what it all means. One powerful aspect of research work is that it not only pushes limits, it eliminates them.

The experience of a researcher during such moments is the reason for all the SRF training. Then as the experience is codified by mentation, reporting occurs on a rapid level as close to the mentation process as possible.

When I was part of the exercise, "I was a Ginn's Plaything", research immersion caused me to feel impelled to act upon every good idea which came to me. I ran around trying to make physically active the concepts which waterfalled my mind ceaselessly. They seemed all really good ideas, of extreme benefit to society, with lasting positive effects. Then when I refused to act out every good idea, the clarity of fresh mind returned, giving me freedom to act as I wished, not impelled by conceptual forces. That exercise was seminal to the Document on Living in the Future.

The exercise I'm in now is similar to that one in intensity, but a more highly developed version. I now have a distance from the play of conceptual constructs, so needed in idea discrimination. I really have no more need for this diary, but will save it for another time.

I saw the artist again, as I was on my way to the Foundation.

Translator's note: As this diary was found together with the documents in the Laborer File, it can be assumed that the diarist was in fact in full possession of this material, and knowingly placed the papers in the metal box for safekeeping. However, handwriting on the back of the papers is not in the hand of the diarist, but that of another researcher.

2

THE SOCIAL RESEARCH FOUNDATION INTERIM REPORT DOCUMENT ON LIVING IN THE FUTURE

CONTENTS

34. Important Insert
    (a) The SRF "It studies the future"
    (b) Willing to Change "To reduce fragmentation"
35. Problem Solving (c)
    "What is relevant data?"
36. Public Forum: questions and answers
    "There are no secret strongholds"
37. Primary Data: Flash Report
    "Onrush of new primary data"
    (a) Living in the Future
    "It is not seen by those who bind information"
    (b) The Song of the 5
    "They completely combine"
38. SRF Declaration
    "In the light of new data"
39. Appendix
    (a) document compilation ecological data
    (b) confidential questionnaire and (c) questionnaire results

Translator's note: What follows is the White Paper Document issued by the SRF in 1983 in closed circuit. For market purposes the Edit/Format Group has considerably reduced this report in the present version, added illustrations, and created a "sample" of the document at hand.
(Illustrations not available at this time.)

THE SOCIAL RESEARCH FOUNDATION INTERIM REPORT DOCUMENT ON LIVING IN THE FUTURE
(feedback version)

1

MARKET TEST SCAN (SELECTED)
(Commentary Feedback #101)
This document for closed circuit distribution only.
NOT FOR PUBLICATION.
Field test: Demographic grouping A-001

INSTRUCTIONS FOR VOLUNTARY VIEWER PARTICIPATING IN MARKET FIELD TEST #101

You have been selected by a rigorous demographic procedure to participate in the SRF prepublication market test scan. Welcome Aboard!

Enclosed you will find your preview draft copy of the SRF Interim Report Document on Living in the Future.

When you have fully completed viewing the document, please immediately fill in the accompanying questionnaire and return it. Your feedback is essential to the developmental stage of the SRF public reportage.

Thank you for your participation.

2

FOREWORD: THE VOLUNTARY PUSH INTO THE FUTURE

(Historical data omitted)

It was after this that the SRF was beginning true experimentation in the lab, and perhaps six months later the SRF reconvened to discover that its members were Living in the Future.

This experience was so different from all previous speculation that it is difficult to report with any accuracy. In fact, one aspect of this phase, hereafter named Phase II, is a difficulty of reporting. Language is clearly inaccurate. The only hope is that through a variety of sources and expressions some hint of SRF activities may be conveyed.

It must be stressed that this is not science fiction, not idle speculation. It is an accurate, clear, concise document.

3
INTRODUCTION

The value of this report is in synthesis. Just as wealth comes by the sorting and packaging of information, so in the synthesis and application of information comes the value of this report.

Nothing is new under the sun, Solomon said. In repackaging, reprocessing and reproducing information the SRF throws new light on old topics.

SRF Commentary: Many researchers, when beginning to communicate phase-shifted comments, have initial difficulty of clarity. These problems make attactive packaging impossible, but they are useful as verifiers of authenticity of reportage. The reporter in this instance has added: The idea of not looking too closely will only lead to error. We are totally this one field without a stop. The whole thing is rolled into a ball and given identity by us. We analyze, repackage, and continuously reprocess data in this holographic field.

Analyst note: How can such a document be considered serious, or a useful tool which could be referred to at a later date? It is a document which is actually totally subjective.

SRF Reply: The definition of subjective is currently under revision to promote individual analysis of specific data by elimination of the personal and private. Definitions of personal and private are also being revised to give a connotation reminiscent of their past definitions, but without the idea of separated individuality.

Statistical information is now shaped and formed to create data to support subjective views. The data collected in this way are organized and disseminated to those who use the results to advantage. This is Common Knowledge.

Common Knowledge has become a manipulatable commodity in the information warehouse.

THIS DOCUMENT WILL BE OF USE TO ANY SOCIAL RESEARCHER WHO WISHES TO DEVELOP CONCEPTS ALONG THESE LINES.

Translator's note: Historians of thought will find interest in the concurrence of this introduction with present popular beliefs. Particularly note the reformat of definitions of private, personal and subjective, some of the SRF pioneering work. However, we are at a loss to explain the last statement (in caps). It has been speculated that this edition of the document contained information and notes not included in the standard copy.

4
THE HUMAN LABORATORY

As in the days of alchemists and the pre-Vedic philosophers, we are forced into individual experimentation on the human being to develop prototypes of all kinds.

It is the duty of those interested in social research to first acknowledge the laboratory available. There is no form of study so useful and ideal.

In the flood of re-run general data, the only recourse for the individual is to become a sorting mechanism - compiling and assimilating according to personal criteria.

This personalized sorting generates meaning from information.

5
HISTORY OF THE SRF - PERSONAL NOTES

While interviewing people who had achieved prominence in their fields, I noticed many were affiliated with impressive organizations and institutions. Many were founders or co-founders of these corporate expressions of their work, and their affiliation with corporate bodies added stature to their cv's.

Deciding that I, too, would do the same, I founded in 1980 an organization called The Social Research Foundation (SRF). The field seemed broad enough to encompass many activities, yet framing a direction in which I was already active as a lay-viewer.

As there is no stopping an idea whose time has come, the rapid expansion of the SRF into a full reality operationally and organizationally occurred almost overnight.

As we now change phase from one reality to another, it is a marketable gesture to embody ideas as corporate entities rather than have them come ignobly from frail subjective unscientific humans.

The SRF has now considerably expanded. I wish to extend gratitude to all those who have assisted this expansion. These are individuals around the world who believe in the validity of subjective expression and analysis. It is to them that the present direction of the SRF is dedicated.

The SRF creed is repeated by researchers and reporters in the field as well as analysts and compilers online. It states that we are dedicated to further Social Research using human experience as the input with artistic expression as the outward report form.

6
INFORMATION SORTING

Using a non-linear approach to data-gathering, and relying on input from sense-data, the SRF also scans periodicals, relevant courses, media sources, such as radio, television, and closed circuit video as well as popular films, theatre, art expressions, and thought and dreams.

Much information is gathered through private interviews of a wide range of individuals and groups. All interviews take place in a relaxed and unstressed context, providing optimum response from those questioned (detailed description follows.)

Once information is gathered (the process is ongoing and continually subject to revision) it is sorted according to SRF criteria. These criteria are also continually under process revision due to ongoing data collection.

It is useful from time to time to come up with an interim report which touches major areas of interesting research before criteria change to such an extent that the previously collected and sorted data is rendered obsolete and useful only in historical retrospect. This is one such report.

7
REPORT FORM

The present document is the first SRF White Paper report format. Usually, SRF reportage is documented in oral form, sometimes as feedback during interviews, sometimes in commentary during a tv program, movie or presentation.

Although the SRF is continually expressing reports in experimental forms, and monitoring response to these, this is the first official interim report on living in the future. Previous experimental reports were in the form of movement, dreams, events, art works, conversations, or even using thought itself as a report form.

However, in an attempt to communicate SRF conclusions to a wider audience, this White Paper form has been selected as the attractive packaging which will produce the greatest audience response (in this case - belief).

The paper is subject to revision and will reappear in revised form at a later date, when feedback has been evaluated.

Translator's note: There has been no other version of this white paper found. It may be of interest to note that indicators imply that the SRF report forms also included ritual, but this was much later in the history of the organization.

8
PRIMARY DATA REPORT 0034

I was going crazy from a pressure which was undefined. What I believed was not helping me to cope and I eventually collapsed in an illness which was related to research stress. Not trusting doctors who have no understanding of social research, I waited it out and really gave up completely.

The SRF asked me to list what I gave up.

1. The idea of getting a job, any job, just to connect with the past.
2. The idea of being an individual who could change society at large.
3. The emotional pressure which laid me flat.
4. The many undefined and unarticulated responses to the stress of social research.
5. Conceptual bases of world-views and their attendant ideas.
6. Time relationships.

> A - It was not mystical.
> B - It was unpleasant.
> C - It was difficult.

Arms, hands, legs and feet were numb and tingling. Head ached, and stuffed sinus blocked all air entering. Thought was impossible. Anxiety prevailed. Then it began to slowly release. Pain entered legs, feet, arms and hands. Nose cleared and headache subsided. The next day, tears and sobbing.

It was necessary to report.

Translator's note: It has been cited in other materials from this time period in global history that many otherwise perfectly "normal" persons did experience a series of inner blows, caused it seems to us now, by the rapid changes which were overtaking society at large.

9

RAGS AND BONES

In the context of an information reality, the culling and sorting of data is of primary importance. When using sources of data such as current periodicals, a reporter can feel like a rag-picker. The high-grade unused information which is accessed by those who are in informational authority is simply not present. Auguries therefore occur by dissection of commonplace sources.

The waves of emotional dream-response material used by advertisers and other salespeople are often predominant. A new kind of research and reportage arises which infuses meaning (by whatever method available) to these predigested information particles.

The clever reporter sees other connections than those intended, and connects these with conclusion from previous sources. A pattern is formed through subjective dissection and augury. The idiosyncratic build-up of world-vision based on external mediating sources becomes in fact an extension of the reporter's personal mind.

10
PRIMARY DATA REPORT 439
AT HOME IN THE ELECTRONIC COTTAGE

What electronic cottage? We couldn't afford to buy all that expensive hardware. But it seemed to happen just the same. Here at home we are Indians of Luxury; we sit around with the coffee on all day. The consciousness brought about through experimentation in the lab of life is consistent whatever the external context may be.

There is much to do. People seem to be unemployed, or if they do have a job it is temporary or could become so. Some are working all the time. Some are not working at all. Some are in a fever pace, then collapse exhausted. Some do nothing it seems at all. There is much to do. There is nothing to do. There is much to do. There is nothing to do. The two electronic cottages sit side by side - much and nothing.

Translator's note: There is a series of versions of "At Home in the Electronic Cottage" collected by the SRF but this version is the only one included in the Laborer File. The following handwritten notes were found on the back of this page:

EL COTT Preprimary Data
We like it/sleep in/ work from home/ out to eat/write/hike/buy food/ clean house/mow lawn/talk/good ideas/watch tv/laugh/stay up late/wonder/make art/ laugh/feed one another/wash one another/embrace/ laugh/meditate/think/water plants/watch the fire/swim/sing/listen to music on the stereo/talk long distance/ think/plan/discuss/get excited/get bored/have visitors/go out/stay in/watch lightning storm/get sick/help each other/read/write/cry/dress/clean/care/tend/ start fires/worry/talk/We like it/sleep in/ work from home/ out to eat/write/ hike/buy food/ clean house/mow lawn/talk/good ideas/watch tv/laugh/stay up late/wonder/make art/laugh/feed one another/wash oneanother/embrace/ laugh/meditate/think/water plants/watch the fire/swim/sing/listen to music on the stereo/talk long distance/think/plan/discuss/get excited/get bored/have visitors/go out/stay in/watch lightning storm/get sick/help each other/read/write/ cry/dress/clean/care/tend/start fires/worry/talk/We like it/sleep in/ work from home/ out to eat/write/hike/buy food/ clean house/mow lawn/talk/good ideas/ watch tv/laugh/stay up late/wonder/make art/laugh/feed one another/wash one another/embrace/ laugh/meditate/think/water plants/watch the fire/swim/sing/ listen to music on the stereo/talk long distance/think/plan/discuss/get excited/ get bored/have visitors/go out/stay in/watch lightning storm/get sick/help each other/read/write/cry/dress/clean/care/tend/start fires/worry/talk/

11
PRIVACY

This question is in many ways pivotal to the entire report. - but reporting is being interfered with by memory - (real-time reportage has the advantage
of immediacy but its disadvantage is interruption)
Quickly dealing with the memory -
(a) The Plastic People of the Universe were a Czech rock band which brought
the people together in the common cause of freedom, for which the players
were jailed. Their cause was the only protest after the Russian takeover which
activated the general public, and this was not for themselves but for the unjust
imprisonment of the Plastic People.
(b) Staring out the window after hearing the radio, I saw a return of the anti-war
riots, of the streets thronged with angry demonstrators, of the people without
roots, anti-society and the young people coming out of high school into what?
No jobs. No future. Anger and frustration exploding everywhere as a result,
nihilistic property damage. This was in 1980 when I heard a radio documentary
on China in the time of the Red Guard. Interviews with former members. Give
us back our youth, they had chanted. Before that, anti-intellectual, they sent
erudite Chinese to communes where the monodiet of yams and constant work
knocked the brains out of them. The thought of North America's voluntary version of the same anit-intellectual phenomenon, with voluntary communes, etc.
There.

Analyst Comment: This report must be made more concise. Subjectivity must
never plunge into personal comment or memory. There must, after all, remain
some privacy.

SRF note: The memories this researcher describes are in fact based on mediated
experience and auguries based on mediated experience, and are not personal
memories at all.

The privacy in the future will be newly created, different in form and
feeling. We can be open, subjective, honest and clear. But private thoughts, inner
life, all that which cannot be codified remains unseen.
Bank account, is that private?
That which cannot be codified will be considered private. That which
can be codified will be considered public information. It is suggested, therefore,
according to SRF data, that persons wishing to retain or create a sense of privacy
begin by finding that which cannot be codified and by cutting identiy with that
which can.

12
PHASE II

Those other research foundations interested in studying the future will find Voluntary Implicity an essence term. Using Fresh Mind to scan data, the researcher often sees that which is implicit, and usually hidden from a viewer who searches within a state of Fresh Mind Exhaustion.

The second step after observation of that which is implicit in events is the entry into the field of that which is implicit.

This means to use Fresh Mind to actually enter and become for an instant that which is implicit.

The explicit, which is the intention of the presentation or event is not considered,

Fresh Mind is very useful as a tool for entry and is cultivated by its recognition.

Voluntary Implicity is often stating the obvious, which has become obscured due either to information overflow or deliberate obscuration for purposes of power or wealth.

13
AUDIENCE FOR THIS DOCUMENT
Addressing the issue of audience-creation, or marketing:

Admittedly, the work of the SRF has at present limited special interest appeal. However, once the SRF work becomes known, SRF will become a household word.

Certainly around the electronic cottage, wired or not, SRF has become synonymous with high-grade information attractively packaged containing just the right amount of absolutely everything.

The question really is, How does this material become common knowledge? Through the distribution of this valuable interim report. The infrastructure is in place and we intend to use it.

Here the information is so attractively packaged it must come to the attention of the general public, although not in the form of this document itself. It could well be that this document (as high-grade information) may have a limited closed circuit impact.

And not through recognizable key personalities either.

It may circulate samisdat only to surface on network television in a completely degraded translation.

14
AUDIENCE II PHASE II

The process of preparation of this document has alerted others in this social research field to co-work with these ideas in a similar vein. The unfolding

of this document is itself its own communication, holographic and total. Not in linear terms but in totality, the Interim report documents a phase shift felt by some social researchers alread and yet to be felt by others.
(insert graph)

Social researchers have in fact penetrated to Phase V, while this report is still documenting the simple shift from Phase I to II, with III overlap. It must be remembered that society at large will necessarily follow the social researchers through these phases. Therefore documents and reports are especially valuable.

As well as communicating to others in the field, such reports send vital information "down the line". The shift into Phase I has become a commonplace experience for many. It is to be seen if documentation from Phase II can usefully affect the social structures to encourage convenient phase shifting without severe social dislocations.

15

PRIMARY DATA REPORT 298
LIVING IN THE LAB OF LUXURY

If you're so smart, why ain't you rich?

Yes, we are living in the lab of luxury with foods from all over the world and items of all sorts surrounding us constantly. Some of them don't work as well as they used to and yes my old pocket calculator-watch is held together with scotch tape but its a good life, all told.

16

THE FUTURE

Clearly, the future experienced by all persons simultaneously will occur over time (as a serial reckoning).

To examine the future, researchers enter the parallel shifted attitude event of "future" and simulate the time-related future. It is a research simulation.

Some researchers who are in simulation phases beyond II and III have communicated that they feel they are at a stage of research in which they create all data, analyses, and compilations which they then report back as "future materials".

Reports transmitted directly without intervening mediation tend to uphold this view. If this is indeed so, the idea of the creation of the future through social research would come out of the realm of science fiction and into reality.

Even Phase I understanding is too limited, however, to recognize the subtleties of matrix-overlap and their implications. Phase II or further simulations are required.

Usually the unmediated reports from future phases are translated immediately into working languages. The language necessarily communicates limitations not indicated at all in the original free context.

It is for a larger number of researchers to actually enter the farther reaches of the field before accuracy can be tested in this regard.

Inklings are our best verbalization for these yet unconfirmed research findings.

17
COMMENTARY ON PREPARATION OF THIS REPORT
by Primary Researcher 1A-43
(REALTIME IS OUR WATCHWORD AT THE SRF)

To prepare an interim report on matters of this nature is a difficult task at best. Problems arise at every turn concerning language clarity. The selection of analyzed data is primary: to choose the most "typical" information which can be most easily audience-accessed. All this under normal circumstances would be easy.

However, as this report is interim, and social research is continuing even as this report is being prepared, the tremendous rapid-feedback processes which the SRF put in motion at its onset often interfere with reporting accurately, for from time to time that which is being reported on is in fact changing due to more current data. It is for this reason that the SRF limited the timeframe in which the document would be prepared to two weeks.

Naturally, the abovementioned feedback problem was considered into report planning. But report preparation has set into action forces of which the SRF had no precognition whatsoever. It is necessary to report these processes as well.

Two factors are recognized so far during the preparation:
1.

(a) The very act of sorting, compiling, and analyzing SRF materials from the point of view of easy audience access causes a revolution in the SRF itself.

(b) As that which had been inner becomes outered, a new inner takes its place.

(c) This process renders all reports obsolete as they are being compiled.

(d) In the search for new non-obsolete prepared or packaged data, the reporter enters this process, outers inner at a more and more rapid pace yet feels the prepared analyzed compilation presented to the audience is outmoded and therefore worthless, ie. not very marketable.

(e) It is only dedication to the field of social research, and recognition of the situation described in the graph chart above, that give incentive to continue reporting and preparing the document.

2.

(a) Through the process described above, the reporter becomes increasingly aware of the realities of documentation

(b) Finding that the shift from Phase I to II has already occurred, and that description of Phase II is best done by inference, the act of preparing an interim report seems to propel the SRF into Phase III at an intense rate.

(c) It could be said that the completion of the document is the entry into Phase III.

(d) As this phase shift occurs, reportage becomes more difficult.

(e) Language problems, concept shifts, and disorientation cause reports to fragment.

(f) As attitudes shift view, data which once had great report significance tend to lose value.

The SRF Pattern Guard will ensure that the document preparation will be seen in "experiment view" and conclusions will be suspended until after completion. It is not certain, however, that Pattern Guard in experiment-view will in fact hold together through this phase shift. If the experiment mode shatters, "moral duty" "public benefit" or some other such obligatory mode will be attempted. Experiment view has had success in the past for all new material events, whereas research has shown that "moral duty" and other such Pattern Guards tend to shift out of phase under pressure.

18

TRANSITION DATA

1. Excitement Phase

New Reporter:

When I first heard about the future, I became very excited. It was true! It was really happening! I couldn't contain my excitement and told all my friends long stories about the effects of new technology on society.

SRF Comment:

This initial "excitement phase" is technology-based and hardware-related. It is nearest to the industrial consciousness and seems to involve a speed-up of industrial values.

2. Rejection of Industrial Values

New Reporter: Then I realized that what looked like tremendous possibilities also had a potential to codify humanity and make fascists of us all. I began to conceive of ways the new technology could be used in an open, conversational manner. I became excited by these ideas, and told all my friends about the incredible potential for good and evil and how it was all up to us or we would be techno-peasants in the electronic world of the future.

SRF Comment:

This probing into the infrastructure base causes a rejection of industrial values. The "excitement" of the hardware phase is tempered and channelled into a populist form of futuristic humanism.

3. No Response
New Reporter:

Trying to encourage people to see from that point of view, I wrote papers and presented briefs and set up classes. I was disappointed to discover that everyone had their own concerns. There was not much response to my attempts to alert and awaken the populace. Most people who were interested seemed to be in the first excitement of it all and wouldn't listen.

SRF Comment:

Still using literate-industrial means leads to little response in the conveyance of ideas based in the future.

4. Abandoning the Linear Approach
New Reporter:

I gave up that line and became interested in visual language and the roots of communication. I began seriously to make art for fun. I was immensely happy, happier than I had been for a long time. I was so relieved to be rid of all those ideas which had bothered me so much and had made me feel that I had to do something about them all the time.

SRF Comment:

This stage of release, or let down, is essential in development, for all linear approach is abandoned.

5. The Future Attitude
New Reporter:

I didn't think at all about the future or about technology. I was as if numb in that direction. All I did was live life, make art. For a time I went entirely without reading. It was a happy time and I looked on the time I was seized with evangelical zeal about technological change as a mistake.
SRF Comment:

At this point, the Phase Shift from I to II is evident. The future which was far away has overlapped the present and in fact become it. The future is not based in hardware, which is only a factor. Research has shown that the future attitude and way of living is very unlike "ideas of the future" held in the excitement phase.

6. Entering Phase III
New Reporter:
About a year after this, I realized I was living in the future and wondered how many others were doing the same. Then I heard of the SRF report document, and added my comments to it.
SRF Comment:
This understanding shows a completed Phase II shift. The desire to once again comment may show a beginning of Phase III overlap.

19
AUTHENTICITY
The document is questioned by viewers and analysts. They ask, "Is this really real or is this really fraudulent?"
The answer must be a paraphrase from the well-known Buddhist bestseller, *The Diamond Sutra*: "Just so, Subhuti. It is neither wholly real, nor wholly fraudulent. Nor is it wholly not real, nor wholly not fraudulent. Just so, it is neither the Interim Report Document, nor is it not the Interim Report Document. "The Interim Report Document" is just the name given to it."
Measurement of the "reality" of the SRF documents must be done in relativity, using SRF criteria. As this report was declared subjective at the outset, all measurement of its truth or falsehood must be made from the vantage-point of an authorized SRF reporter. Therefore, the SRF certifies unquestionably the absolute veracity of this document at the time of compilation. However, the SRF retains the right to, at any time, adjust data, analyses and conclusions according to revision needs as they arise.

20
TRANSCRIPT 443
The process of transcribing previously used thoughts or old thoughts in their original style renders thought useless for Social Research.
Social Research is an up-to-the-minute expression of present thoughts, as faithfully transcribed here in this commentary.
Attractive real-time thought-packaging renders Social Research extremely useful in the information marketplace.
Subjectivity with lack of personal vantage point combines well with a hard-edge reality base to provide no-nonsense compiled data which affords easy audience access.
It is a friendly fact form which will soon catch on.

Documentary Print is the SRF's favorite info-style.

Catchy, factual and real-time, it erases all previous thought-paks.

Even Pattern Guard itself is now being prepared in this light factual tone. Watch for it!

21

HIGH GRADE INFORMATION

Those who read Social Research report documents such as this tend to search for high-grade unused information which has not yet been attractively packaged as re-runs. Such viewers will be disappointed by the slick style and lack of raw data in this interim report.

Nevertheless, this particular document is, in fact, ushering in a new era of report documentation, particularly as it applies to the Social Research field.

No longer will the social researcher be taxed with pages of undigested data. By taking a comprehensive subjective view, the SRF has leapt into the wide new field of Personalization. This affords vast resources of data, already attractively packaged in a personalized form. Thus, subjectivity creates high-grade information.

Even when the original data sources are "common knowledge" personal filtration of Social Research data transforms low-grade multi-use information into high-grade "special interest" information with the bonus of attractive packaging.

Recycled informational components can reappear again and again without causing Fresh Mind Exhaustion thanks to the personalization of the subjective view.

22

GUIDELINES FOR STUDY

An Experienced Researcher - Lecture Notes

What is Social Research?

Even researchers themselves often ask this question, sometimes as often as those outside the field. The old saw, "What would life be without coffee? But then what is life with coffee?" can easily be repositioned to refer to that activity which, for lack of a better term, is called Social Research.

In the Social Research Foundation definition, the field differs from sociology, anthropology, demographics and psychographics in that the study occurs in the lab of the researcher's life itself, with a view to the future. It differs from psychology and other related Californian disciplines in that it is subjective while remaining impersonal (i.e. privacy is always maintained). Although it shares some connection with pre-Vedic yogic experimentation (in that the human being IS the laboratory) it is also similar to alchemy; Social Research, being futuristic and media-aware, also works within the ecology-matrix laboratory of the society at large.

It is, in short, a new and promising field of research having little or nothing to do with previous disciplines, except by resonance. Researchers are not recruited through universities, and only a few private foundations such as the Social Research Foundation are active to date.

Many individuals, or lay-viewers, are interested in the field, but it is only through the public disclosure of interim reports or involvement in report commentaries that a lay-viewer can officially enter the status of researcher and benefit from the information accesses which are the privilege of that station. Such information is extremely high-grade.

Perpetual sufferers of Fresh Mind Exhaustion are simply unsuited to research. Even less suited are those who seek such exhaustion as reverse-stimulus. Only keen researchers with the ability to recognize and develop FM (Fresh Mind) can begin as lay-viewers to observe the phenomena of present data.

Compilation and attractive packaging require further will and analysis attributes which are usually natural to researchers with FM tuning.

One small bit of data recognized through Fresh Mind is considered extremely high-grade and very marketable to compilers and analysts. Social researchers can, by analysis of prepared mediated materials using FM create new high-grade data. This is a useful skill in these days of information overplay!

Attractive as the field may seem to be, it features many drawbacks and stresses, such as exemplified in Report 0034. A multiple-matrix researcher, working full time in the future encounters difficulties in sorting and analysis, as well as stress in simple information holding.

The language problem inherent in communication from one future phase to Phase I or even all the way to non-researchers (i.e. the general public) makes clear and accurate information reportage as stressful as the original analyses.

This is where FM can again come into play. FM offers clarity where there is confusion, calm instead of anxiety, and replaces future with present, communication with conversation. All information release must occur in some FM mode.

Perhaps this overview of some of the activities can implicate the essence of Social Research and in some small way assist a lay-viewer's appreciation of this valuable document.

23
TIME MATRIX

The time matrix is a field which requires constant participation for existence. Those researchers who do not participate in this conceptual structure often fail to report back within the time-frame previously agreed upon.

Without the time-matrix, can there be agreement? Naturally, is the reply of a seasoned researcher. Experimental proof is not available, however, as this researcher seems incoherent in reportage at this time.

24
NOT HUMAN INTERACTION

It must be emphasized that this SRF Interim Report Document is not reporting on human interaction. It refers to a state/stage of human life which will define its own interactions. Reporting on phase shifts experienced in the lab, it references subjectively to notions of time and space within SRF criteria only.

The idea or notion of time is central to the future as above described. For a researcher to enter the central core of a phase shift by applying voluntary implicity, through FM tuning, is the purpose of research preplanning. However, the difficulty in reportage from such a vantage created the need to imply rather than state the facts which are reported back.

Thus, clothed in the limited mental structures of concepts familiar as icons to any lay-viewer, the SRF document reports not on the seen and known and familiar, but on the overlap phase shift which is indescribable in conceptual form.

Translator's note: To clarify, the research simulation "Living in the Future" consisted of several phases which occurred naturally in the "Lab of Luxury". The reports included here so far document a shift from Phase II to III in real-time. They do not reflect society at that time, but individual views which have been analyzed and prepared to produce this report.

25
UNCLASSIFIED REPORT DATA
(Source unknown)

> melting of previous valuables into nothing at all
> complete and utter day to day quality of life
> poetry-defying subjectless objectless matrix
> easy laughter, sweet tears
> embrace
> trees
> O sky_____

Translator's note: Although the document states "source unknown" there was some indecipherable handwriting on this page of the Laborer File, which seems to indicate that the author was indeed known and identified.

26
GUIDELINES FOR STUDY
Research Stress

Often research stresses are not noticed until reporting, when researchers find various physiological and psychological imbalances can occur.

This condition often discourages the report aspect of research, but for the sake of other researchers it must continue.

Remember, the only proven effective relief of research stress is reportage.

27
UNCLASSIFIED DATA

SRF Disclaimer: This reporter appeared to show symptoms of stress leading to intensified personalization (NEGATIVE 43) and refused to continue preparing the Interim Report. It was negotiated to include this personal statement, in order that the work continue as preplanned. SRF does not maintain the views expressed in this unclassifiable report.

I quit! I'm sick and tired of having the dance of the soul, which is what reporting actually is, being put through the contortions of this bureaucratic jargon and false governmentese. I can speak for myself and I don't want to use these silly "approved concept structures" any more!

From the time I began to be interested in learning, I mean really interested, I was always forced and channelled into the jail for thoughts which our most intelligent-seeming people seem to think is the pinnacle of achievement. Well you can all shove it!! I've certainly had more than enough of your posturing and pretence. Even my resentment and frustration comes out expressed in YOUR language. I quit but I can't escape.

That's really what I am so furious about. I feel I am speaking, writing, and thinking in a language which is not my own, not spontaneous. It is a second language, not a mother tongue. If I look back far enough, I can remember that mother tongue, that beautiful delight: the spoken language, my expression.

Now when I have to speak I am not fluent, but I can write very clearly. That is why I do the work I do. But it makes a hole somewhere and a deep yearning feeling. Everything is tied up in these structures which really are pretend and we all know it is so but don't do anything about it.

When I was a child I actually used to believe that people who couldn't read or write were more like animals. They were stupid, of course, and couldn't think or invent anything. Most of all, they didn't have refined feelings like we do. I didn't know then about the Nazi reading Rilke as he sent people to the gas chamber.

I can't stand it any longer and I'd rather be one of those stupid animal people because they do have feelings and more, they know something more. I need to learn it all, all the nuance of life by living life, not reading or writing it.

How absurd to be reporting on the future! I quit. Reporting is a difficult and thankless job and reporting on the future is worse.

I must confess that this idea of quitting and returning to simple emotions and thoughts is just a literary device. Once a reporter has begun work, there is no turning back no matter how appealing that may seem.

But I do wonder if all the allergies people have these days are not from pollutants at all but are instead repressed sobbing.

Analysis is so complex! Thank heavens for Fresh Mind!

I can't really quit, nor can I make SRF into a cruel unfair employer. We are all part of each other around here and as one of the foremost researchers in the field, I owe it to Social Research to continue.

I simply reapply the Pattern Guard.

(But I wonder: How can I have true FM with Pattern Guard applied? Perhaps SRF must adjust criteria.)

Have other researchers been here before me? Perhaps this is a useful stage and can be applied as a modifier to future experience. I therefore insist that the SRF include this document in the interim report: the information is subjectively valid.

28

INDIANS OF LUXURY

It is clear to many reading this document that underlying its purported purpose is a force which must originate in the future and which is in fact forcing research along certain lines. To those who have observed this phenomenon may also have come the obvious conclusion that by combining certain aspects of the text, the central experience will be inferred.

Viewers who are themselves researchers will note the invitation to do just that, realizing from previous experience that such action produces a "message" which appears to come from the future itself and which directly applies to the viewer at this moment.

Making use of the beginning of this document and following key phrases which randomly appear important to the scanning eye, we produce:
"Living in the future, not directly affiliated in any way, Indians of luxury certify unquestionably the complete and utter day to day quality of life."
or
"Prototypes of all kinds and most interaction take place in homes. Time relationships and all statements are subject to revision. Unmediated reports give typical information on the potential for good and evil."

29
GUIDELINES FOR STUDY
Reporter Transfiguration (Note to Reporters Only)

Reporters are more subject to sudden transfiguration than are research-ers, who are free to come and go at will. Research, free form and experiential, allows the participants a wide range of prototype being, without accountability to any particular criteria-set or Characterization of Persona Package. Reporters, on the other hand, face complex translation problems. Ideally, the best reporter is a researcher also, and a researcher who does not report is useless to the Social Research field.

REMEMBER:

1. A reporter who knows the material gives accurate reports.

2. Many reporters who translate research data fail in attractive packaging due to difficulties in understanding what the research is actually about.

3. Researchers who act as reporters are more accountable, making factual the experiences which are otherwise uncommunicated and therefore ephemeral or private.

Thus researcher/reporters are ideal.

Sudden transfiguration, however, often plagues reporters who are also researchers. In such a case, the report becomes dislocated from previous docu-ment style. Often, the reporter feels like quitting or not longer continuing in the future. Pattern Guard fails.

This crisis situation is usually not lasting. Most researcher/reporters return to report mode fairly rapidly, but after such episodes, they tend to be less able to report without commentary. The SRF is required to fully monitor all behavior to ensure correct reporting is still in occurrence.

30
GUIDELINES FOR STUDY
Notes for SRF Training Lecture: The Problem of Personalization
For reporters -
-Difficulties include:
- personalization while retaining privacy
- personalization can go too far, making documents useless for Social Research but perhaps meaningful to reporter's friends and family
- yet lack of personalization leads to objectivity which renders dead data
- balance is needed - up to each reporter to achieve.

Motto: ALTHOUGH ALL DATA IS PERSONALIZED, DON'T TAKE IT PERSONALLY

31

UNCLASSIFIED REPORT DATA
Can it be Possible?

If researchers make reality, we could be lifted from the darkness by the imaging of a world: by light. See, a person bends, sobbing in darkness. It is too slow there - the light moves quickly. The dance/shimmer/purity of life is there, in darkness - image it. Even in the immense poverty of the drabness, the colorlessness. O children, the povertyborn. The person bends sobbing in darkness, the tears have no stop. For light shows - and will not relent. Compassion.

32

PROBLEM SOLVING (A)
Research Involves Individual Experimentation

As research involves individual experimentation, a social researcher can feel alone in the research as it is being done. Affiliation with an organization like the SRF does little to eliminate the key feeling of being alone as the first to enter the particular area under study.

Interestingly enough, this feeling occurs even in the preliminary stages. Yet it is well known that many social researchers have crossed those areas, some long ago. It has therefore been confirmed that social research involves a feeling of aloneness.

Once research is under way, naturally a researcher also gathers data from reports of others in the field. Here, also, the individuality of reporters becomes all too apparent.

Although all researchers agree totally on the field of research and often on the situations raised and the conclusions formed, each is entirely unique. Research has shown that two reporters in identical fields (as much as can be inferred by comparison) can report back entirely different messages. These individual subjective privatized views add great richness and variety to the social research field. It does mean, however, that once a researcher enters SR seriously, there is no turning back into group consciousness as previously understood.

33

PROBLEM SOLVING (B)
Change in the Sense of Time

The phase shifts, attitude changes and other attendant phenomena surrounding the work of Social Research do little to expose the most subtle transformation: Change in the sense of time.

On this point, almost all researchers agree. There is a definite shift into a sense of time which is like that experienced by children of another preliterate culture.

Yet, at the same time, all other time experiences are also present and available according to need (just as all phases are simultaneously present).

One problem facing researchers is just this experience: being in actuality during research in this "timeless/timefree" state, yet with reportage and "daily life" still continuing in reckoning-based time. This is one research stress which clear reporters find is most amusing to play within.

34
IMPORTANT INSERT
For Reporter/Researchers Only
Memo
(a) The SRF

The SRF is, contrary to the feelings of some reporters, not a fascist force. It is completely benign. It is absolutely without regulations, without outwardly enforced unchangeable criteria, without autocratic tendencies.

Because it studies the future, and because it is an experimentally-dedicated foundation, the SRF can appear to have some of the qualities of possible futures, particularly due to the subjective nature of research. But these are simply passing experiments. The SRF is literally free. It enters contexts at will, and is free from contextual control. Within its own range, the SRF can control all research contexts, but this is done with complete cooperation of all those working in the SRF.

To address the situation of reporter breakdown:

It must be clearly stated that under no circumstances does the SRF force reportage or research. Everyone is free to come and go at any time. Neither does the SRF demand lack of human impulses or humanity in the actions and attitudes of reporter/researchers. It does, however, expect a job well done. This, plus research stress, can cause reporters to feel forced. The forced feeling, combined with the feeling of aloneness common to social research are simply part of the psychological difficulties of the field.

(b) The SRF is Willing to Change

The SRF follows carefully the experiential data as researchers report back, and ensures that this data is analyzed to adjust report criteria. Even within a report such as this one, where Pattern Guard in experiment view has been put in place in real-time until the end of the report period, there is possibility of change.

If informational data garnered through research is radically "new" or extraordinary enough, or from other phases, or could create a breakthrough in Social Research itself, then naturally the SRF will open its doors to the possibilities such discoveries can offer.

Pattern Guard is only in place to reduce fragmentation. If data prove that fragmentation is preferable, then PG will be removed.

This is the SRF position at present.

Real-time reportage will now continue as preplanned.

35
PROBLEM SOLVING (C)
Difficulty in Research Mode

Often while conducting research, reporters find difficulty remaining in research mode. Aside from contributing factors discussed above, there is a Fresh Mind Exhaustion unique to the research situation.

The question, "what is relevant data?" comes up again and again as the overflow and replay continue nonstop. Often researchers just stare blankly ahead, or choose a low-level stimulus in order to relax the brain.

Response variety is the key, and the multilevel matrix of research and report modes help immensely to remove fixation, replacing it with information circulation once again.

REMEMBER:
(a) High pressure is relieved by reportage.
(b) Low pressure is relieved by increased stimulus.
This is common knowledge.

The clear researcher senses which balance, (a) or (b), is appropriate and employs them to create full productivity with little loss of report.

The white paper report form, a tight mode indeed, is much more stressful than other forms as it tends to box in a researcher. More balances need to be applied in this situation.

36
PUBLIC FORUM
Questions and Answers

From time to time, the SRF is asked a number of specific questions by lay-viewers, other researchers and the general public. During the preparation of this document, three such questions were received.

1. What is the purpose or benefit of marketing social research?
2. Is there anything which is not informational?
3. Is there a distinction between pure and applied social research?

The SRF gives a clear and revealing answer to question 1, based on present data analyses.

The marketing policy of the SRF, stated briefly, is that attractively packaged information should be available to all, regardless of their status and interest.

For the benefit of humanity, and to close the widening gap between the information "haves" and "have-nots", the SRF produces reports from time to time. In an information reality, marketing means distribution and distribution means viewers. The SRF data compilations are made available to viewers at a reasonable rate.

Freedom of information does not mean that information is free. It seems high-grade information is very costly these days. The SRF offers high-grade subjective information at low-grade information rates, distributed and marketed as if it were in fact common knowledge.

Do not be fooled! Implicit within all SRF reports are all the tools an interested lay-viewer needs to produce many other similar documents based on subjective reworking of existing data. Such information is extremely high-grade. It allows ordinary viewers without high accesses into the game at a new level. It makes the game more complex, and necessitates new rules, new judging of structures. The SRF encourages entry by all into the future phases.

Marketing social research data compilations prepares the public to participate in the game and alerts hoarders of information that there are no secret strongholds.

37
PRIMARY DATA
Memo
Flash Report

The SRF has taken the unprecedented step of entering a phase yet to be discovered by any other research foundation. (Perhaps this is not exactly so, keeping in mind the "feeling of aloneness in research" problem).

There occurs now a tremendous upheaval of all previous SRF data, analyses and compilations. Many old files are simply being junked due to incompatibility with the onrush of new primary data, much of which has to be handled in an entirely different way.

It was the preparation of this interim report document which precipitated the change in the SRF, one which is presently occurring from ground level to all others, and which now seriously affects the SRF's network of correspondents and regional report bases.

At this point the news is still breaking. So far, the SRF still exists, but in a considerably changed form which has yet to be defined (if ever).

New Data subjectively gathered concerning living in the future has agitated the SRF so severely that readout is not clear at this time.

Report scans so far read:
(a) Living in the Future

It can be categorically stated that all transformation occurs through ritual and that all ritual is art. All art is therefore transformational.

The future is now inhabited by technocrats. These beings understand one another but the lay people do not understand them or their works. From this lack of understanding the technocrats produce tremendous wealth. The lay people have little choice but to obey. The only non-technocrats who see this situation shall be called artists.

The artists are the people who balance and clarify the future by pointing out exactly what is occurring. This is done by inference and by laughing in the game. The artist's fluid mind wins out over information-clogged wealth acquisitors.

The rituals performed as art transform knowledge into action again. It becomes free energy outside conceptual jails. Artists perform their rituals with sly awareness, wearing the clothes of the mind they expose. This means that they become technocrats, but false versions. They use the tools the technocrats thought were theirs. They laugh at the tools and play with them. This ritual ensures power is not only in the hands of the technocrats. Because they are blinded, the techs are unaware of this process.

It has been going on for some time now. It is not new. "Nothing is new under the sun," Solomon said.

The techs are in check while art is in the picture. This art is not necessarily prettier, it is in other clothes, and the disguise is the art.

(b) The Song of the 5
Art and science join
The techs are left far behind, counting imaginary wealth
Humanity begins:
We live like cave people in love and luxury
We report back
We dance as earth, as water, as fire, as air, and as ether
We do not stop.
We make rituals through human beings who are capable of holding our power and from whom this power does not escape.
Someone is holding 5 snakes. They are being tame.
Those we make rituals though are the artists
They are our colors
They are gold, green, red, blue and grey
They twist together as 5 snakes
No one sees it
The artists make the snakes stand up and dance
They stand very tall
These 5 snakes do a version of primal life. We open our mouths, we drink from the cup which they form of their own bodies.
The cup is white
It is very bright and humming in pure sound
The 5 are present and make us animate
We are now looking to them

When artists make ritual to release concepts which have bound power, these 5
come bursting forth
There is homage, there is rejoice
When a concept shatters, one or more of these 5 come forth
There is homage, there is rejoice
When many concepts shatter, the 5 stand up and dance
There is homage, there is rejoice
The artist is in white and the 5 obey
They go in and out of one another
They completely combine
One is straight
One is wavy and downward
One goes upward
One is zigzag
One emanates
They worship one another by combining in human forms
This is a dream of life, it is beyond the future
It is not seen by those who bind information
It is seen by the artist who laughs
Look at letters on a page - some are long, some wide, some zigzag, others wavy
and downward. Some point upward, others across

38
SRF DECLARATION
In the light of new data now received, the SRF declares:
1. The future is out of the hands of the technocrats and in the hands of artists
2. To be an artist is to burst all energy from its information-concept jail
3. Social research and art are one
4. There is no declaration of truth
5. A good spy lives his cover
The SRF will continue forging new inroads in the field of Social Research. Watch
for the next Report, in which the SRF examines conclusions formed from the
new data and outlines further this present direction.

39
APPENDIX TO THE INTERIM REPORT DOCUMENT ON LIVING IN THE FUTURE

(a) Document Compilation Ecological Data
1. The document was compiled from August 6,1983 to August 20, 1983.
2. Geographical area of research: North Temperate Zone: (a) mountains, (b) inland beach, (c) parkland, (d) prairie.
3. No major city was visited during compilation.
4. Temperatures ranged from 5 degrees C to 37 degrees C.
5. Climate: hot dry, hot moist, cool moist, cool cold (mountain evenings only).
6. Range by day: sun, cloud, thunderstorm, wind.
7. Range by night: moon new to full, clear, cloudy, wind.
8. Media climate featured: US planes sent to Chad, Wargames begin in Honduras, BC workers demand rights, Melanin discovered central to all neural processes.
9. Number of persons interviewed or who otherwise shared the event: 21.
10. Correspondence received for duration of compilation only: Canada 15, USA 10, Australia 2, New Zealand 3, Sweden 1, Mongolia 1, Holland 1.
11. Long distance calls: 4.

12. Compilation occurred:

In SRF office	- 40%
In car	- 5%
In restaurant	- 5%
On beach	- 25%
In bed	- 20%
Other	- 5%

(b) Confidential Questionnaire

Market Test Scan Group A-1
Now that you have had the opportunity to prescan this document, please respond to the following questionnaire.

A. TRUE OR FALSE
1. I believe the SRF document to be true   T___F___
2. In the future, all people will be social researchers   T___F___
3. The conclusion of the document is fiction   T___F___
4. Most people will not understand this document   T___F___
5. I understand this document   T___F___
6. In the future, phases will be abolished   T___F___

B. MULTIPLE CHOICE

1. This document is   ___(a) easy to read and understand
                                       ___(b) difficult to read and understand
                                       ___(c) somewhat difficult
                                       ___(d) mainly easy

2. This is actually   ___(a) an epic poem
                                       ___(b) a send up
                                       ___(c) a factual report
                                       ___(d) an art object

3. The document   ___(a) applies to me directly
                                       ___(b) has nothing to do with me at all
                                       ___(c) applies to people I know or have seen
                                       ___(d) refers to no one I know or have seen

4. I am presently   ___(a) living in the future
                                         ___(b) living in the present
                                       ___(c) living in the past
                                       ___(not applicable)

5. If you answered (a) to question 4, please respond -
I am presently in   ___(a) Phase I
                                         ___(b) Phase II
                                         ___(c) Phase III
                                         ___(d) some other phase

6. The future phases as described   ___(a) are accurate to my knowledge
                                               ___(b) are inaccurate
                                               ___(c) do not apply to me
                                               ___(d) cannot be measured

7. I consider myself to be   ___(a) a researcher
                                             ___(b) a reporter
                                           ___(c) a lay-viewer
                                             ___(d) an observer

C. COMMENTARY

1. Does this document perform a useful function? Yes___No___
Why?

2. Does this document present a view of life in the future? Yes___No___
Why?

3. Would you recommend this report to your friends and co-workers? Yes___
No___
Why?

4. Is the information implied through this report clear? Yes___No___
Why?

5. Do you feel this document should be widely distributed? Yes___No___
Why?

6. Did you enjoy reading this document? Yes___No___
Why?

D. APPEAL SCALE

Rate responses 1. most preferable, 2. all right, 3. not preferable.
1. What form of packaging is most appealing for this document?
          Book___ Magazine article___Pamphlet___Comic___As is___
2. What graphic additions would enhance appeal?
          Photos___Charts and graphs___Illustrations___ None___

3. Who should this document appeal to most?
          Educated employed___Uneducated employed___ Educated unem-
ployed___ Uneducated unemployed___ Overeducated unemployed___

E. REMARKS _____

Thank you for your participation.

(c) Questionnaire results
Translator's note: The results to this questionnaire are uncompiled in this Laborer File. This seems to indicate that the market test scan was really of little
interest to this particular branch of the SRF, or perhaps that the beta testing was
simply a screen to mask the dissemination of ideas which would otherwise have
been "officialized" by SRF headquarters.

Code 431 - Information Grade: 7 - Do not remove from file

THE SOCIAL RESEARCH FOUNDATION
SUPPLEMENT TO
THE INTERIM REPORT
DOCUMENT

Contents

THE SOCIAL RESEARCH FOUNDATION SUPPLEMENT TO THE INTERIM REPORT DOCUMENT

Code 431 - Information Grade: 7 - Do not remove from file

1

INTRODUCTION

Although results of the market prepublication beta testings have not yet been compiled, the SRF has concluded some new findings in regard to living in the future. What follows are several Primary Data reports, Interim analyses, and selected reporter quotations which came in after the market test scan version of the interim report. They may be of use to compilers at this stage. Reevaluation of the SRF criteria and the SRF itself is also outlined.

2

SOCIAL RESEARCH FOUNDATION REEVALUATION DATA
(For Internal Circulation only)

The following idea-clusters may be of assistance to compilers and analysts:

(a) Results

As results from beta testing of the Interim Report Document on Living in the Future start pouring in, the reevaluation of the document begins. Again, it was true for Aug. 6 to Aug. 30 in 1983 but present indications have leapt far beyond that limited view. (See previous collected and analyzed data)

Some respondents felt constrained by the language (as did reporters) and it must be noted the Phase III and beyond reportage is without the heavy bureaucratic phraseology, yet may be even more difficult for most viewers to understand. Of course, stating the obvious requires specialized language if that information is to be profitably marketed.

(b) Packaging

The SRF will take all reports from future phases and publicize them using market skills in order to alert the general public with useful information. However, indicators read that such packaging as in this report form tends to lack user-friendly attributes which the common public has come to expect. Even the direct news-reader style did not meet with clear positive response, scans have shown.

What, to the SRF in future phases, seemed to be the Ideal Package was in fact considered less appropriate or marketable by many who were scanned.

The resulting dilemma can be stated thus: If, as viewer beta tests suggest, the White Paper format is not effective, then how can this information be presented in a marketable form? Certainly the forms "novel" or "video" would lose the document as it is now expressed.

(c) Rationale

The SRF stands behind Documentary Print as a valid art form for these reasons:

1. Most people employed today and using writing skills are encouraged in their work to present briefs, proposals and even letters in this chatty yet impersonal style.

2. This style has not been recognized as a subjective expression, yet more writing occurs in such a logical mode than in any other.

3. It is art to work in the clothing of the past culture phase.

(d) Mediation of Language

The mediation of language in all communication lends the feeling of the language to the communication. In Documentary Print, the rational impersonal mode is an impediment to the expression of individuality, feelings and personal art. Thus the use of this mode can be frustrating to the viewer who tends to search for such qualities. A viewer, however, can see that Documentary Print is not what it appears to be.

It must be made completely clear that it is because of the restrictions imposed that this language is ideal to point out the restrictions inherent in our social institutional formats.

(e) Art
(Section omitted)

(f) Statement

Documentary Print speaks authoritatively and appears to be true. News reports use a remarkably similar style.

(g) Premises

It has been shown through beta test results so far received that the basic premises of the SRF have not been fully explained to date. Also clear is the fact that subtlety of report often causes confusion, or worse, escapes notice. The subtlety will not be made flat for easy observation. However, as a concession to viewers, the SRF will include an extensive glossary at the end of the document, and will lay out the principles of the organization here.

1. The SRF is an independent organization dedicated to the field of social research.

2. It is based on the premise that subjective information processing is as valuable to human society as (so-called) objective data.

3. The SRF firmly believes that conclusions drawn from subjective information processing are as valid as objective ones, more so in some cases.

4. The SRF is dedicated to spreading these ideas through art.

(h) Conclusion

SRF organizational scheme involves several field reporters who scan their own experience and report back their experience to SRF headquarters. Here, the material is compiled, analyzed, synthesized and presented to others in the form most appropriate.

At this time, the SRF is committed to Documentary Print as its most useful form of reported expression. This decision will not change despite the repeated requests from viewers for more accessible/multiple-meaning/right brain forms. At this time there will be no SRF novel, poem, video, music, drama, dance, ritual or image forms.

The SRF wishes to stress and point out, through putting on, the limitations of Documentary Print and what that does to the mind and expression of those who use it and who believe it. Any frustration experienced by viewers caused by the use of this mode will only add to the point the SRF intends to make: that print is not a valid form any longer for the gathering or assessing of information, nor does it have nuance enough to express what is needed today - the subjective view.

Translator's note: This material was not included in any other found SRF files (aside from the northern data). The introduction appears straightforward, but indicates that the reports are Primary Data and the analyses are Interim. In this way, we suppose, otherwise "unofficial" information could circulate internally in the SRF organization. Much of what follows is of great historical interest, as it not only documents the workings of the SRF itself, but it also includes interesting extraordinary unclassified data.

3

PRECONCLUSIVE DATA: OTHER CHANGES IN THE DOCUMENT

The Phase III experienced by researchers is a busy, active phase, non-linear yet more mental than the previous visual phase. It seems Phase III is a combination of I and II, with aspects of both, much like a union of left and right brain modes. There is a crucial difference, however, which has been described by researchers:

1. "Phase III, although bearing elements of both I and II, and excluding none of their attributes, is in actuality more unlike them"

2. "It is a logical wasteland where things no longer make sense, yet they do after all or seem to."

3. "The potential seems enormous and it is a state of power."

4. "That which is envisioned from the point of Phase III analysis becomes manifest in some way on some other Phase."

Those researchers discovering the creation of present experience through manipulating future elements seem to have little interest in doing so, except in matters of altruism or livelihood. In this activity, the elements of earlier phases are subjugated, controlled and used much as animals were trained by primitive human beings.

SRF Comment: Phase III is a negative state which produces the appearance of power but in actuality it is empty of interest. As such, the SRF will discourage further Phase III research.

4

ANALYSIS 5A: REPORT FROM PHASE III

The evolution of humankind through future phases appears guided or led but is totally dependent on individual participation to a degree which is more intense and involving than anything else - except, perhaps, love. [Comment: fuzzy-minded, inconclusive]

The holographic model of a united core of all is a way of looking at things which is actually also limited. [Comment: reference unclear]

The remarkable individual develops as a prototype of possibility with or without assistance from those in his/her group or tribe. The tribal metamind of which the developing individual is an active member opens more and more as this individual progresses. [Comment: what is meant by "tribe"?]

This progress occurs in all directions. Up, down, to the front, to the back, to the sides, and along all axes in between these. This creates the sun, or an image of the sun. A human being in this mode is a remarkable individual. [Comment: where did that notion come from?]

The sun shines thus in a multiple matrix of interfaces with others of similar brilliance. As the rays of growth and development meet those of others, these interstices create new stimulus for further development. These rays meet at small stars which communicate back to the individual who is a sun. The sun becomes more intelligent from such contact. [Comment: this has nothing to do with research as we know it.]

Intelligence of this sort transfers quickly and unimpeded throughout the being of the remarkable individual. It is all unseen and quick. It is a world of light exchange and creation. Those who have not begun this work do not radiate clear enough beams to begin to exchange information on this level. [Comment: excessive aggrandization]

The play of the mind is the sorting of this internalized light-created intelligence, which develops at a faster and faster rate, making normal sorting processes impossible to use. The person become stupid-seeming as this exchange is sorted and assimilated, but when it is completed, a normal life continues as if uninterrupted. [Comment: this report not of use. Check reporter for loss of Pattern Guard. Discard document]

A person stares across an abyss and there seems no reason to jump across. Yet the person jumps. When there is no observer, it is impossible to tell if the person lands or crashes. Because from the person's point of view, he does land. But it is not land known.

This human person is comprised of many people. They are all one enormous human being. It is vital that this human being begins this jump.

THE MIND IS JUST A BIG PLACE, DON'T YOU EVER FORGET IT, KIDS!

Translator's note: The above seems to be an example of Phase III reporting, which is juxtaposed with the following report.

5
ANALYSIS 5B: REPORT FROM PHASE III

Often reporters who are unsure of their facts will cloak them in mystical terms - vague and nebulous references which reflect a hazy romanticism. Nothing could be further from the truth, nor more misleading to the viewer. Far clearer to viewers than hazy neo-mysticism is the use of symbols.

Through the ages reporters have found symbols work best to get their message across and firmly anchored in the hearts and minds of the public.

Reader satisfaction comes easily when true symbols charged with unfoldable meaning are transferred by wordcode. In today's rapidfire world, encoding by symbol saves time without losing impact. Try them yourself!

Caution: Just because it is seen, perceived, written or spoken, with enormous conviction at that, does not mean that it is true.

6
Quotations from a Conversation of 3 Senior Researchers (edited)

R1: The human sickness from which we suffer is a loss of intensity, a loss of symbolic ring echoing through our being.

R3: Well, the demand for fresh information will cause us to seek deeper into the roots of human knowledge, unearthing symbols, signs and messages which will be trotted out in new garb and rediscovered to public adoration.

R2: This process must be accellerated. We could be saved from the shallow stupidity which we are hurtling toward by the intervention of the past.

R3: Perhaps, for the value in studying these phenomena and in perpetrating further the ideas embodied here is in accelerating human evolution.

R2: But the ideas of evolution and devolution are always simultaneously passing one another.

R1: Yes. Now the old tribal mythologies are no longer stories to us. The tales we tell on television are repeating over and over our mythologies, with various characters acting various versions of the same elemental tales. What are these tales to us? Who are we telling them to? Why must we remember them?

R2: The lives of artists must be dedicated to this essential retrieval. And all artists are involved in either evolution or devolution.

R3: Yes, all art is then presented as a fresh new phenomenon but it is only effective if it creates evolution or devolution. The artist creating devolution has a more difficult life, but does clear the way.

R2: I see the beginning of worded art coming when words, treated as objects, are arranged and ordered as if they were items to be juxtaposed and then viewed. The combinations are viewed and seen, not read. This gives readers the new role of "viewers" and also opens doorways into the centre of all created word.

7

SPECIAL REPORT: R1

(a) Findings Related to Action in Holographic Reality

What interests researchers today is the question of action and change. Given this view of reality as holographic, how does change occur in a world where cause and effect are not connected in a linear way?

Our present society is an all pervasive bureaucracy. A bureaucratic alchemy works to develop the remarkable individual who can penetrate this seemingly closed system.

Tribal society is a closed system; the workings are established and set to run. These workings come out of the tribal dream. The dream is hidden by symbols. Life looks simple. Beneath it runs the dream. Only certain trained self-disciplined individuals manipulate the symbols which alter the dream. They do this to heal the sick, to celebrate the seasons, for food, for war, for glorification of the greater entities of the dream. To enter the realm of Manipulator of Symbols is to become representative of the tribal being, and to lose personal identity. Those who take this role become one with all those who have gone before, yet they are remarkable individuals in their own right. The gifts of remarkable individuals are channelled for the good of the tribe. Those who try to change conditions outside this structure are clowns, but have no real power.

In present reality, there exist multiple representatives of varied societal elements. These fragment the power and use varied symbols in diverse ways. Symbol manipulation is used mostly by those who have little self-discipline and who are hungry for power and wealth. Thus the public is manipulated by their own dreams.

To make change, a change in the dream equation is required. To substitute dream for dream, so the power changes. This is done subtly. New dreams take the place of the previously programmed fragments and the people respond, through recognition, to the new dream equation.

The dream equation is the status quo. The change required is the introduction of recognizable dreams which were not before considered valid. These enter the system by means of symbols.

It must be emphasized that the symbols are placed in such a way that the former dream context allows their introduction without turmoil.

Frustrated individuals try to use force to create new realities. These do not work, nor will they last. In the diversity of present society, new symbols can introduce other dream forms easily and without stress. Gradually a resonance may begin to exist, considerably changing the entire field. To change the field will naturally cause another dynamic. This will effect change in a holographic reality.

Quote: "For some time now I have wrestled with the question of how to create change in a sleeping society which is not active. Apathy, video-induced bad dreams, petty worries, all combine to make the public powerless and uninterested in social change. Those who do attempt it seem to partially fail as the mode used does not acknowledge the cohesive complexity of present day life. The dream is too powerful."

(b) Senior Researcher's Comment

Those who penetrate the dream find it difficult to alert others; verbal and written language fail.

But the application of symbol language changes the context entirely.

There are manifold symbol systems which can be applied to thought, giving space for thinking to be multilayered, interactive, nonlinear, totally holographic.

Holographic thinking is required in order to make change in a society which is holographic. Very often people are fooled by the outer organization of a social system. For example, if in the future a fascist influence took hold through various future developments, people would feel a hopelessness and inability to make change. Most would become simply satisfied with what is there. But in reality it is obvious that the dream behind the seemingly ordered state is not cause and effect at all. It is a scream of fear of chaos. A true World Being recognizes this state, then manipulates the symbols to alleviate fear.

(c) Delineation of the World Being

Representatives of the tribe who manipulate symbols in present time can be called World Beings. These individuals love humanity to such an extent that they leave their petty minds and allow themselves to become remarkable individuals dedicated to the service of humanity.

Such sentiments are generally unpopular, and are seen with cynicism by those who keep certain deathdreams currently circulating through the consciousness of humanity. The deathdreams generate wealth by the sale of products to alleviate fear and suffering.

The sentiments of a World Being are usually contexted as "religious" and therefore without application to the "real" world, and without reasonable substance. This framing method usually stupifies the effect of symbol manipulation except in the small areas of popular support for the particular "religious figure" so contexted.

8

SOCIAL PHENOMENA

Social phenomena rise to the surface for a period of time, then fade again. While they occur, they appear to be all there is, reality. These fads now come and go with increased speed. The moment of prominence and ultimate decline have less and less meaning attached to them. To what, then, is meaning attached?

The power is to be seen behind the scenes, actually manipulating these risings and fallings. Public awareness is manipulated from one focus of attention to another. It mechanically continues on in patterns, almost like man-made seasons or weather. This is our environment: a dense, external push-pull world which increases in velocity and intensity, an ecology based in mind, in dreams.

However, the normal viewer rarely participates in the world so expertly shouted at him. Instead, he experiences a parallel life which is usually seen as paler, less colorful than this other more "real" world dream life. Man tries to change his experiential world into this "real" world dream life by purchasing products or by living according to prepackaged available ideals, but he usually continues living a pale parallel life despite these additions.

There is a secret. The experiential life also has power when lived with another dream to motivate it. The mechanical daily life becomes infused with power when this shift occurs, for when a person creates his own dreams to guide life's track, the old deathdream has less and less power.

The new dream is introduced into the total shared "reality" context by an extraordinary and yet simple method: a person truly living that dream. Visualization is not enough.

The person who lives a life guided by these self-created dreams becomes a living symbol of that dream. That dream is now firmly anchored in the sphere of human life and is available to all.

A variety of active dreams, lived totally, produces a healthy world culture of diversity and fascinating interest. Conversely, mono-dream cultures are prey to social manipulation and are basically unhealthy.

9
VOLUNTARY STATEMENT BY ARTIST (selected)
[selection omitted]

10
INTERNAL PROBLEMS AND REORIENTATION STRATEGY
Definitely Not for Circulation - Classification X)

(a) Letter
        I began to think, to reevaluate my reasons for entering into social re-
search. It was disappointment, and a need to understand. It was frustration with
present reality and a need to impact it somehow. It was almost a perverse need
to get back at the society which has created the frustration, disappointment and
need to understand.
        I learned how to tune myself to the social research frequency and used
that tuning as a filter of experience. This then was translated as research documents.
        I am ashamed now of the observations made through this nihilistic
filtration system and am now completely devoted to a rehabilitated lifestyle.
        This is my letter of resignation to the SRF and from any further re-
search.
        Do not try to contact me again, and never again try to establish re-
search links.
SRF comment: It is very difficult to keep up encouraging contact with researchers-
ers in the field. Often the fieldwork is lonely, stressful and, for long periods of
time, boring. Many fully trained reporters do burn out, reevaluate research in
that light and give it up. Of those who do quit, some 50% find they must return,
25% find they can no longer function in society and become reclusive outcasts.
Only 25% of those who leave for a better life actually are reintegrated into society with few aberrations.

(b) Message from a Former Reporter (excerpt)
        When the stresses from the future collided with the material needs of
the present, I was forced by circumstances to take a job in the past. All memory
of the future phases I once experienced is vanishing in the limited constriction
of the daily job grind. If reportage had not occurred when it did, there would be
no trace of future experience.
        Even now, I wonder if the terms past, present and future are at all ap-
propriate to the exploration referred to as social research.
        I will continue filing reports from the field to the SRF, but cannot
guarantee their relevance to the SRF criteria for topic control.

It may be, however, that a depth can be discovered through the combination of past reportage with future outlook.

Second Message from Former Reporter (degradation of material has already set in)

The new $4.50 items are all in stock but we have run out of the $12 gold thread version. All items are reduced by 15% except those which are reduced by 10%. Be sure to lock all doors and double check these afterwards. Do not go to the back if there is anyone in front. Please remember to note all calls and read them back later.
Is this of any use to you?

(c) Internal Commentary

Reports from the field have indicated that there are problems in the SRF which would cause unrest if not dealt with. These all centre on one particular point: the report process itself.

Most reporters indicate "future" reportage to be impossible and desire to work back to the "present". The SRF, always flexible, is pleased to accommodate. Reportage henceforth will centre on "present" and the stress of future reportage will be eliminated.

(d) Reorientation in the SRF

As with all institutions in these times, the SRF is undergoing a major change. Research was being conducted solely in the future, which led eventually to a break in staff relations, and a certain amount of unreliable reportage. Since the new directive, some reporters have come forward with admissions that they have been known to falsify reports. Others confessed near mental breakdown. It is obvious that such a situation could no longer continue. There are some seasoned researchers who have chosen to remain in the future, but some were so shocked by the work there that they resorted to taking jobs in the past.

Ever-monitoring the sensitive research situation, the SRF was aware that the problems had reached a proportion which could only mean radical change.

Regrouping at headquarters, researchers, reporters, fieldworkers and report staff met continuously for over a week to hammer out new guidelines. Of course, the guidelines were based on the directive the SRF had established in the beginning of its operations.
The guidelines now are:
1. To emphasise the subjective as a valid information-sorting process.
2. To study social phenomena and their relationship to individual experience.
3. To express research findings to the public at large.

Those who wished to continue in the future were mandated to do so, while those wishing to report on the present were equally supported. However, it was decided those working in the past cannot submit worthwhile reports at this time.

(e) Time and Space

The SRF is no longer interested in time-related reports - such designations as future, past, etc. - but is far more interested in experience-related reports, without reference to the time-base, whether real or theoretical. In this way, the SRF exemplifies the adage, "There is nothing new under the sun".

The experiential base requires a new report method. At present, all reporters and researchers have returned to intensive training to prepare for this new method and approach. Even the SRF cannot imagine what the results of this training will be.

Briefly outlined, so far we have:

- training, including lectures, workshops, simulations
- field-testing with follow-up workshops and lectures
- trial work in teams with daily evalautions
- field work begins in earnest

This shift of focus has set back the work of the SRF somewhat, but recovery should be complete in a few months.

New reporters have voluntarily approached the SRF, indicating that the new method is right for the present time. Had management not been flexible, this radical shift could have seriously damaged many involved in the Foundation, and might have split the SRF irrevocably.

(f) Research Method

Of course the masks of time: past, present and future and the lineations of space: here or there, still exist, but more as metaphors than as inviolable realities outside mental constructions.

Present mode is the imperative. To be in the present percept mode is essential.

Now we are more and more uncertain about that vague line where white becomes black and black becomes white. We play in that interface to create an entire world.

STATEMENT: This synthesis of present understanding is documented in print extension for private viewing only.

4.
MISCELLANEOUS DATA &
UNCATEGORIZED PAPERS

Contents

1

DOCUMENTS FROM REPORTER 3A - UNCLASSIFIED

People wonder "what is happening?" as the information flow reverses and goes instead from right to left. To accurately report, I would have to write in a language which is visual, which is total, which has no as yet recognizable form. This report is a translation from the experiential to the understandable, from life to dead wordsymbols which still carry a bit of the fragrance but can only refer to experience.

Furthermore, this report is not time-based, for time code is no longer relevant. Yes, it is still a report on the future. I chose after all to continue in the future while others chose instead to be in the present. But to me this "future" is like "the golden age". It is, in other words, progressed aspects of now. As now shifts seemingly along the time-coded gridworld, we progress to this evershifting matrix of "future".

Delighting in observing these dancing lights, researchers begin to forget the purpose of Social Research itself. At such times, the idea of future loses its true nature, which is as a catalyst to now and to reality formation through creative perception.

So what? It must be remembered: speculative reporting and bedazzled researchers have no place in the SRF. It is only through accurate reports by sober research that the creative perception can accurately occur.

2

DOCUMENTS FROM REPORTER 7C - UNCLASSIFIED

MA the mother Matrix

Art is the Answer - Baldly stated, the entire report hinges here, in this one brief statement.

Art is the Answer and those who have bravely taken the step OUT of CULTURE into ART CREATION begin to understand fully the meaning of ART in these times, and in the future.

INVOCATION TO ART

The Balinese statement, "We have no art, we try to do everything well," is often repeated. Why do we continue to repeat this? It is simply an invocation.

As the propulsion moves progress aside to reveal further prospects, we stand outside culture to observe creatively and step into that observation with great ease.

SRF Comment: Reporting has now begun. The accuracy is validated. Phases abolished, the report seems to indicate a sidestepping of culture to create art. The reporter seems to have sidestepped even the SRF here and may be creating art solely and without sanction either socially, culturally or economically. The SRF is willing, as always, to take a chance on new reporting for the sake of greater understanding.

3

FUTURE STATIC SOCIAL STRUCTURE - PRELIMINARY ANALYSIS

SRF Caveat: The writing of the future is actually that - it is a creation, one of many, which collide and fuse and eventually create a future which is present.

Before our culture took precedence, the future was static and part of the tribal dream. In this state, future generations were in fact former family members, and life patterns remained similar. Different conquests, weathers, climates and the rise and fall of natural cycles would make a means of marking change, and what we call past, present and future. However, the marks were slight. Compared with our frenetic accelleration of experience, the tribal dream life seems static. Interestingly, the speedup we now experience leads directly to that very static social structure, to that timelessness.

It seems inevitable that we are socially heading toward a static tribal social structure with visual communications and highly stratified status lines. Along with this comes a lack of social mobility, restricted educational opportunities. But the old guild system, the father-son lineage will not apply. It is not yet clear what the lines of power will be. Money will define class, but not money as it is presently understood. Information access will be more likely to open doors, rather than family affiliation, occupation or address, although these will also be an influence.

In a static society there is a tremendous stability and an emphasis on ritual. To see a future which includes individual freedom as well in this stable society seems very difficult, using present criteria for "individual freedom" that is. Yet there could be such a development. With the family structure broken instead into groupings based loosely on place, occupation or other interest affiliations, as well as friendship and kinship bonds, there could be a greater independence of individuals.

People could be seen as coral in a coral reef, creating an exoskeletal social structure, with social freedom within that structure but remaining held by the coral type in which they have that freedom.

Women will be independent individuals, their children being similarly free within the static stable exostructure. States will change by rituals. Commerce, trading, all arts, will each have their world, or society. Walls will exist between groups naturally created, and will not be considered "bad" but will be considered necessary and "good".

Children, after a certain age ritual, will choose their group affiliation. At other times, certain groups will allow changes in members, but those in some groups will never transfer over to others. Some will be nontransferrable. The groupings will occur for many reasons besides vocation, location or interest. They may also refer to color, belief system, or physical characteristic or handicap. Groupings could be according to talent or potential. But always the groups form according to social need. The persons in groups may live alone, but more likely will be in small kinship nodes, maternally based.

Often liasons will form and shift according to affinity but always the group remains.

The coral exostructure is formed in this manner: dyads and individuals and small clusters live together or separately in places of choice. These "homes" are temporary housing which shifts according to conditions and need. An individual, dyad or cluster will move many times, in no particular set pattern (ie. migration is not necessarily seasonally based) but according to criteria from larger group impulses. These units are based on individual freedom or maternal ties. These will be referred to as Group 1. The Group 1 participants only interact with other Group 1 units in their larger interest group (Group 2).

The larger interest group (Group 2) is based on the criteria listed above. These groups are sometimes encouraged according to location but most often have an economic, informational or cultural-artistic basis. Within any Group 1 group, members are constantly in touch with one another but rarely in touch with members of other groups. They are, in this way, sealed off from many others and do not even understand their premises.

The Group 2s are large, spanning the entire world sometimes and the Group 1s of which they are formed communicate according to need and wealth. Within some Group 2s there is constant contact one to one. Other 2s are not in touch with others in their group in their entire lifetime. It depends on affiliation, need, interest, and the group type.

There are no individuals outside this description. Those who think they are alone, without a group, are also a group, but without contact with one another. In this case, the individual's role in the group is to maintain aloneness and separateness at all times.

Individuals define themselves by their Group 1 affiliation, and often by the Group 2 designation, of which the Group 1 is a participant. Members and groups are very rarely aware of the validity of other group goals, values, or ideals. Except for the Group 2 Elite, all of whom share an ideal of unity and hold an overview.

These group affiliations occur seemingly spontaneously, with no "membership" or particular entrance into a group. They are like the communities, tribes and nations of the past, or like the professions, or demographic groupings, which seem like natural world views to those involved within them. In fact, these groupings are the world to their members. And the meta-groupings, the Group 2 level, creates the coral exostructure of the society in which these various types live and move.

(Notes deleted.)

This society is global. Static. Stable. Based on information in a way not yet seen. There are no large institutions but many versions small and large of need-filling organizations within Group 2 structures which address the needs only of the particular Group 2 membership.

There is not really a question of "happiness". There is love, art, compassion, pain, care, misunderstanding, everything. But striving toward happiness as a personal goal is unknown. A small group may find a thread of such thought, but it is not a prime current.

Many many things taken for granted today are unheard of, unthinkable, impossible to comprehend.

All-at-onceness commands full attention.

5
ADVERTISEMENT PLACED BY SRF IN LOCAL NEWSPAPERS AND CURRENT PERIODICALS WORLDWIDE

A Specific Message to YOU, the overeducated unemployed:
Can you envision the Social Research Foundation?
Can you see the data flow, the sheer information brought to SRF headquarters each week?
Is this a reality to you yet?
Have you seen the reports being compiled, the de-stressing meetings, the training sessions, the recruitment strategies?
Are you aware of ever having met a researcher or reporter in your everyday life?
Do you feel you might have what it takes to enter the field of research yourself?
If so, please reply yes or no to the following questions.
You just might be a Junior Researcher!

The Questions

1. I find myself standing back and observing in situations where others seem totally involved.
Yes___No___
2. I can stay up to all hours when I am enjoying myself.
Yes___No___
3. A daily everyday life seems boring to me.
Yes___No___
4. I do not enjoy participating in mass crowd events.
Yes___No___
5. In most situations, I am a good sport.
Yes___No___
6. Sometimes, I feel I understand everything.
Yes___No___
7. Often I will stay home rather than go out.
Yes___No___
8. I wait for the moment when I can really show them.
Yes___No___
9. I don't care what others think of me.
Yes___No___
10. Even when I speak directly, I often must repeat myself.
Yes___No___
11. I am often clearly understood without having to say much or explain myself.
Yes___No___
12. I like most people.
Yes___No___
13. A change of scene is usually good.
Yes___No___
14. Most people prefer stability.
Yes___No___
15. I express myself well.
Yes___No___
16. I complete whatever I put my mind to.
Yes___No___
17. I have a keen eye for details others don't seem to notice.
Yes___No___
18. I seldom dream, but when I do I always remember my dream.
Yes___No___
19. Sometimes I feel I have a special talent, but I don't know what it is.
Yes___No___
20. I want to help humanity somehow.
Yes___No___

Try these simple questions and send Your Unique Answers to The SRF Recruitment and Training Section 4 in your area!

5

HILL TRIBE REPORT

Contents

1. Introduction
2. Hill Tribe Report Notes - Unedited
3. Hill Tribe Research Report A
4. Cultural Transition
5. The Patterns
6. The Return of Ritual
7. The Idea of "Individual" as Transcendent Goal
8. Pre-Conclusion to Hill Tribe Report
9. SRF Comment
10. New Patterns
11. Official Interim Report on Hill Tribe Gathering
      (a) Although tribe members....
      (b) The peasant class will accept no work....
      (c) The aristocracy have few beards.....
      (d) The aristocracy keep to themselves...
      (e) Food is communal, served....
      (f) Aside from ceremonies...
      (g) In ceremonies, the populace....
      (h) Peasants also enjoy...
      (i) Repression of artistic expression...
      (j) Nature is very important.....
      (k) This same gathering place....
12. Debriefing

1

INTRODUCTION

Often, a social researcher must journey to another country for comparative sociological data. Files are then sent in, some by line feed, others as reports, which are compiled later after debriefing.

Briefing notes: Hill tribe anthropological data is gathered by involvement. Notation occurs sporadically. It is difficult to write linear thoughts from the viewpoint in which these thoughts have exploded.

Poetic imagery comes close, but is not convenient for data retrieval at this time. It can be difficult to surface thoughts under such conditions. Rhythm is essential to develop the correct atmosphere. "Immerse yourself, become them, report back."

Translator's note: It appears that this section of the Laborer File includes much pre-format material, and is therefore of interest to historians as it demonstrates the codification process of the SRF. The unedited notes, combined with debriefing information, the official SRF conclusion, although accurate, may not be at all what the reporter in the field intended.

2

HILL TRIBE REPORT NOTES - UNEDITED

Preparation for the journey into the Hill Tribe gathering: I was chosen by the SRF to investigate anthropologically this gathering of late 20th century hill tribe members. Scattered throughout urban and semi-urban areas, members travel to a remote gathering place to practice the customs of their people.

I was chosen to go as one of them, to study from within and report subjectively on their superstitions, customs and beliefs. Briefing involved the simple instruction: immerse yourself, become them, report back. Although SRF training has prepared me for almost anything, I am still curious and filled with anxious trepidation concerning what will be asked of me, what they do together, and how I will be able to report as I go along in it. I can't wait to find out.

I'll be staying with a sympathetic friend of the SRF while I acclimatize for a few days, then... its off to the hills to meet the hill tribes!

***

Now at the bus waiting to go and I find it impossible to imagine what the gathering could be. The friend of the SRF tried to make connections for me, but these tribes are elusive and slippery to hold. We could not make contact while in the city.

***

Identification of hill tribe members at transportation node: Easily recognizable by their use of gay colors in fanciful designs, members of the hill tribes gather at the bus. Those without characteristic clothing patterns are identified by musical instruments and a general attitude which cannot be worded.

***

Although it is necessary that I report, I realize that if reportage is subjective, then how can I report without betrayal of the confidence of my new friends in the tribes? Not wishing to betray the confidences of my generous hosts, I am thrown into a profound anthropological dilemma. The answer seems only this: that my involvement must be total, my reportage compassionate, and I must always sacrifice honesty for kindness.

***

The people are peasants, it seems. One woman wears bright orange with golden flecks for the occasion. A man, in striped hat, has all he needs in 2 sacks. He offers me juice from a worn container, and smiles his toothless smile to all. He is very loving and eager to help. He is in this country illegally. She is more withdrawn, unused to travelling.

***

I was incorrect! The members on the bus are not at all representative, for those who are now at the gathering are, for the main part, assimilated and much more able to interpenetrate the mainstream of society as we know it. Many I would never suspect as being tribe members.

Speaking to one, I realized that I had missed the real gathering of the hill tribes which occurred a month ago with 20,000 in attendance. How could the SRF have missed it? The little 150 gathered here seems paltry in comparison. Her report on that large gathering is as follows:

Mostly by word of mouth and intertribal communications, the place of meeting is made known. From around the world, members gather and form villages according to interest, affiliation and belief. They live their lives, set up camp, and sit by the fire. Then on a predecided day and time, silence descends on all the members. They drop what they are doing and all meet in a central place, in concentric circles. Afterwards, they return to their villages where great celebration begins. Song, dance, and councils meet in which each person has a say. Then, when the time is done, they all pack up and resume their lives outside.

***

This meeting is different. This meeting has changed my analysis of hill tribes. Perhaps even the briefing the SRF gave me, short as it was, was inaccurate - being founded on a figure-ground principle which actually has no premise.

It can only be said that although hill tribe members participate, all members are not hill tribe per se, although they may ascribe to some hill tribe beliefs.

I will try to discover some of their beliefs. Being here, with them, makes me, a senior researcher, feel like I too am one of them. But then, isn't that exactly as it was intended to be, when I first took on this assignment? Subjective reportage. How can there be subjective reportage when there is no subject, in that the more I become involved, the less of me there is to report. As "I" disappear, so also does the object of my reportage, they are interdependent, subject and object.

Hill tribe report will no longer continue. Such an analysis would prove completely pointless at this time when participating in the gathering brings such interesting insights for broader research concerns. I will address this report to these concerns as influenced by participation in the consciousness of the hill tribe.

3
HILL TRIBE RESEARCH REPORT A - FROM UNEDITED NOTES

Social researchers who have observed future cultural trends see them from the seeds in which they are currently simply background to an older trend which is foreground.

The future can clearly be "predicted" by simply observing the seed as it would be if in the fore. The seeds of future are all present here and now. They can be especially observed when people are looking behind them and a researcher looks ahead. These words "behind" and "ahead" can be taken literally. What was will be again or better said, the culture of long distant past will become present culture which will be the beginning of another era. The transition from culture to culture is what the reporter will now address.

CULTURAL TRANSITION
Seeds of cultural transition can be clearly observed by the following signs:
- they seem to echo the distant or ancient past
- they are very interesting to us and seem new
- they hold, in art, shapes, sounds and forms familiar and unfamiliar
- they sing of something in our bones or hearts or dna
- they seem to be signs of something

Those active researchers who are involved in creative research encourage and stimulate cultural transition.

They establish the lines along which the culture will evolve and then firmly guide the transition of each of the arts, religions, social forms, etc. along these lines.

The lines are created in space, and form themselves through loving thought, concentration and imagination.

Those active researchers who have taken on the role of "creative director" in their field of work will align forces necessary to the development of this work.

It is a grand gigantic play of which few are aware.

In fact, most researchers themselves are unaware of the meaning and impact of their work.

5
THE PATTERNS

The patterns formed by these activities are codified by research organizations and perpetuated as norms.

To some, the patterns and the norms which follow as superstitions, customs and beliefs are seen as "natural developments" but they have always been the work of active researchers acting as independent agents of research organizations of the times.

Perhaps they have worked in religious contexts, or in legal, often as lawgivers or as teachers of humanity. In whatever form the work is the same: evolution.

Cultural transition is very real and is occurring at a high velocity at this time

6
THE RETURN OF RITUAL

Ritual takes a high place in the coming times with emphasis on genuine ritual transitions rather than ceremonial pageantry which will also become more popular.

As it has been said, "In this way we rebuild the foundation of form on earth which has been so very damaged by the wars."

7
THE IDEA OF "INDIVIDUAL" AS TRANSCENDENT GOAL

In the future, with evolved group consciousness, the idea of "individual" will become a transcendent goal.

In a shared field, the so-called "individual" consciousness will be a rarity.

In progressing from separated individuality to shared awareness of consciousness, humanity passes into what the SRF calls "the future".

However, in that state, the goal becomes united individuality, or the art of personality, not simply a uniform glomping together.

Individuality as a transcendent being involves the high art of personality.

Here, the "person", as the individual becomes known, is given a real chance at performance of life.

Acting is the main lively art which comes into play, although music is also primary.

Dance, implied both through movement and music, occurs spontaneously, while poetry is every spoken word.

Of course, the picture would not be complete without interest in the visual arts, manifest in symbolism, color and shape.

All these combine to express the individual person, who, by being, demonstrates the arts in the highest art form, the art of personality.

8
PRE-CONCLUSION TO THE HILL TRIBE REPORT
The report concludes that biological solitude will only give way to extended enhancement. This means: Sliding by words into extended enhancement can only end in wordlessness. Such ending brings immense peace. The peace is the development of new phases of life which sparkle through to form, by the grace of the manipulators of the dream.

SRF Comment:
Although this statement was clear to the researcher at the time of reportage, it will have to be clarified before the full report is distributed generally. Perhaps the research stress in this case has been too much. Incoherent reports are useless to us. MONITOR THIS RESEARCHER CAREFULLY.

9
SRF COMMENT
Hill tribe research clearly correlates data from other sources gathered by SRF reports worldwide. Indicators show great interest in global culture, coinciding with specific personal goals. Emergent patterns include individual artistic expression but with relatively few individuals in the group actually performing, aside from those tribally labelled "performers". However, small cells of interest do evolve art expressions, but with exceptions these are of no genuine cultural value at this time.

Researcher comment: According to the SRF, cultural value refers only to those efforts, processes or products which induce cultural leaps or "progress". The leaps do not progress in a single line or in a single direction but in all directions simultaneously, allowing the HUMAN entity as a whole to dynamically pulsate new expression. These expressions are usually innovations in past/present language forms. From time to time a tremendous shift can occur which allows a complete and certain transition. New languages evolve to express greater dimensions.

The SRF research-report methodology cannot, using documentary print, express or intimate the evolving linguistic forms which are true indicators of cultural transition.

10
NEW PATTERNS

Social research is a most accurate tool for the discovery of patterns and the description of these patterns. The sooner patterns are recognized and that recognition is expressed, the sooner new patterns are able to form. The patterns which are recognized then become components of social language and as such are recognized by more and more people and groups until they are part of the culture, or common knowledge.

Art is the creation or bringing into recognition of new patterns. It is also the enhancement of old or early forgotten patterns. Ritual is the use of patterns to transpose realities. The relationship of art and ritual forms a pattern in any culture which reveals a great deal about the life of that culture. One can read the age of any culture by the analysis of its art and rituals. Of course, it is always a continuous process of change and interchange.

At the end of a cultural cycle, ritual becomes rote and fails to transpose reality for the majority in the society. Art then tends to act as a cleansing tool, literally smashing those blocks which have formed through pattern repetition.

There are some patterns which retain coherence and power in a variety of cultural situations and times. These patterns seem inherent in humanity and form our symbolic pool for thought. The symbols rise and fall from use according to need and association. Artful symbol manipulation carries the highest charge.

11
OFFICIAL INTERIM REPORT
ON HILL TRIBE GATHERING
COMPILED THROUGH
SRF ANALYSIS

HILL TRIBE DATA COMPILED FROM REPORTS FILED FROM THE
FIELD: PRE-COMPILATION ANALYSIS

1

Although tribe members were not readily identifiable (aside from some members
of the peasant class), they all became similar and revealed that hill tribe characteristics were simply hidden beneath a more socially acceptable facade. When
these characteristics reveal themselves, tribe members refer to it as "being themselves". Some even refer to it as a religious or mystical experience.

2

The peasant class will accept no work, no authority over them. They work only
when they must and drop jobs at the slightest whim. They seem more interested
in what they call "expressing themselves" and usually laugh at and ridicule all
who are employed, although most of them are actually temporarily employed
most of the time. Most were educated or trained in socially accepted schools,
trades or skills. However, their hill tribe affiliation will not let them use the skills
they were trained with. It is the custom in hill tribes to laugh at such training
and to look back on such times as mistakes or bad experiences. The majority of
the hill tribe is made up of this peasant class. They wear gaily colored patterns
on their clothing, and tend to wear shoes which they can slip on and off easily.
Costume for the women involves pants beneath calf-length skirts or dresses,
with large shawls or wrappers to cover them. Many twist cloths about the head,
in a wrap or turban style. Hair is usually left long and flowing, although some,
for practical purposes do have shorter hair. Men wear loose pants with patterned
tops or completely nondescript earth colors. They, too, use the shawl-wrap, but
do not cover their heads. Some particularly special men will wear ikat patterned
sarongs, with necklaces, and hair fashioned in a topknot decorated with flowers.
Hair which is not very long is kept midlength with beards being the average
norm. The beard does not indicate anything in particular (ie. married or unmar-
ried) but the grey beards are usually long, indicating "elder" status in the hill
tribe.

3

The aristocracy have few beards and those who are bearded are very clean. They tend not to wear the flashy colors and patterns favored by the peasants, but sometimes wear one or two tasteful items of value. For ceremonial occasions, the high aristocrats wear simple robes of white or gold over their plain clothing. Most of the aristocrats are considered successful in the socially-accepted greater society, in which they work or create well-marketed works of art. They seem bent on developing group consciousness in the peasants while they themselves have the freedom of individuality. At this gathering were both priests and priestesses who remained withdrawn from the main crowd and who were only visible to those with whom they had specific appointments for consultation.

4

The aristocracy keep to themselves and make little effort to contact the peasant class although the peasants clamor to be noticed by them. In ceremonies some favored peasants are drawn into the centre to receive the blessing of the aristocrats. Yet the favored class feels a need to constantly instruct and correct the peasants, often rudely admonishing them for their stupidity before allowing them to look into one another's eyes. But they must never look into the eyes of the aristocrat without his/her permission, and then only in the sacred circle of ceremony. These rules of behavior are accepted as normal by all and appear unquestioned.

5

Food is communal, served 3 times a day from a common outlet. A gathering by all but the priests and priestesses precedes each meal. There announcements are proclaimed and a blessing is sung by all the company. People then push together through the doorway to the food. Children are allowed to eat first, while many loiter behind to talk with one another. Only the peasants and a few token egalitarian priests eat at this time, sitting at tables where they will. Conversation occurs during meals, and is the usual panache of gossip and discussion of personal health and the physical body. Many of the peasants are completely fascinated by the working of the body and devote as much time and attention as possible to this art. Volunteers clean all the dishes for everyone after the meal is finished, and people walk away to attend to their other needs.

6

Aside from ceremonies, folk dancing is the most popular activity during such gatherings. Singing and wearing traditional costume, people dance in circles and in twos or even threes. Musicians accompany on stringed instruments, and beat out hypnotic rhythms on hand drums. In such states as the dances induce, people whirl about with great enthusiasm. However, custom dictates that they never laugh or comment to one another, but only share the group consciousness of the dance itself. After each dance, the dancers remain still and silent, as if involved in some communication which is without word or gesture. Concentric circles surround the musicians as the dancers sing and perform elaborate movements. Interestingly, the movements are not "dance gesture" as we commonly understand it, but are changes of placement of the entire body, lifting and lowering the arms, spinning the whole body, meeting and matching different partners. Individually there is little or no dance gesture. It only makes sense in a cultural way when involved in the group or circle. Often people wear their finest garments and widest skirts for the dance occasions, but this custom has been supplanted in later years by the prominence of ceremonies which many tribe members appear to prefer.

7

In ceremonies, the populace wear their finest clothes, wash and adorn their bodies (even the feet) and obediently line up outside the ceremony hall. When the priest and priestess are made ready, the hall doors open and the company processes in a regal manner around the room, chanting a sacred phrase whispered to them upon entry. Musicians play a variety of instruments in one corner of the hall and people are assembled according to rank and privilege. Those of various categories begin to intone sacred phrases while the priest and priestess pace through the hall creating a holy atmosphere. This builds until the ceremonies of blessing are made to occur as the company moves as one body in a holy trance. When the ceremony has been completed, the people are led out of the hall, where they find their shoes and celebrate in small parties until dawn. These ceremonies have become quite popular events and often are preferred over folk dancing.

8

Peasants also enjoy sitting by the fire in the hall singing songs, or exchanging items such as crystals or hand drums. They are kind to one another but have a manner inherited from the aristocrats. In this social habit, the peasants copy the aristocrats, pretending to be cool and standoffish to each other. However, friendship circles break open often to receive others and there people are very loving to each other. They touch one another often and hug in greeting as a matter of course.

9

Repression of artistic expression not sanctioned by the aristocrats occurred on one day. Art concerning theocratic stupidity was placed one morning in the dining area, rendering the dining area an effective small gallery. By mid-day, all remnants of this event had been removed. When asked, many hill tribe members had not seen it, nor were they aware of it. Those who had seen it were mostly disgusted, and few, if any, understood the artist's intention. The artist never identified himself.

10
Nature is very important to hill tribe members. The idea of nature as totally good and welcoming predominates. They use chemicals to ward off insects, and enjoy lying in the sun appreciating the natural gifts.

11
This same gathering place in the woods is used repeatedly throughout the summer by successions of tribes with varied intentions and goals, some theocratic, some recreational, some ideological.

12
DEBRIEFING

Researcher "debriefing blues" often follows this type of anthropological research which, by its very involving nature, causes varied side effects when researchers leave that area of study and instead re-enter the world at large.

Debriefing usually takes place immediately upon exiting the anthrofield, before the researcher "returns to himself,",as it is referred to.

After debriefing and before report compilation, the researcher may feel lost or anxious. This pause between modes can best be handled by senior researchers who have the ability developed over time and again to switch personage at will. For beginners or intermediates however, interruption during transition can be very psychologically dangerous.

Of the debriefing process, little can be reported, except that the verbal "retelling" (often repeated many times to many persons) can eventually deaden the information to such an extent that the reporter is exhausted and loses any interest in the report. Subjectivity is lost. Dream analysis then comes into play. For example, the reporter's dream notes given here:

1. My hair is flaring up. I place my hand on my head, and it makes my hair catch fire! I am not afraid, it doesn't burn. However it flares out. I try to pat it down with my hands but it flames out at every touch. I wet my hands and drip water on my head, smoothing the hair and there is no more fire.

2. There are two groups of four women standing around an outdoor fire. They are identically dressed. One group is wearing coats from the 60's - winter coats with back belts. The others are wearing identical raincoats from the 60's. When they say who they are, I nod in acknowledgement. It is ritual information.

3. A mass or interwoven sea of transforming faces in darkness. Are they ugly? They are not beautiful. One becomes the other in plastic motion. I wake and say a repetition which averts evil influence. I wonder why this is happening. There is no answer. The interwoven images are simply coming and going. It is a language of image and it reveals thoughts from prehistory in modern clothes.

4. No "dream analysis" can interpret the "meaning" here, for the images themselves are their own meaning. The dreams are vivid and bright colored, but in a darkened light. I know that when they stop, I will miss them, but when they happen, I want them to stop.

(SRF comment deleted)

6.
THE SRF IN TRANSITION:
COLLECTED FOUND DOCUMENTS

Contents

1

INTRODUCTION

Translator's note: It appears that some time during and directly after the Hill Tribe Project, the SRF underwent a major transition which is scantily documented here. Among the papers found were these fragments, which had been recopied for further study. Their origins are not known, nor are the researchers involved described any further than what we present here. It does appear that the fragments were being copied or reproduced for some purpose, but we have little data to confirm this, and none to indicate just what such a purpose would be.

2
MARGINAL NOTES
    As I compile this particular analysis for general usage, at another work station a similar researcher is doing the same thing. Perhaps she is being used as a checker, and has been given identical data to compile in her own way, for comparative purposes?
    The SRF has broken down considerably with injuries to many members and change of direction. The few with whom I have major work are still close to the original ideas, but the others feel that WE are the renegades. Research has shown that all organizations, whether biological beings or nations, all come to this.

3
MEMO
    We will meet to decide our new direction in a month or so. Given world attitudes and the hot political atmosphere, it is imperative that research occur on correct lines rather than be used unwittingly by other forces.

4
EXCERPT FROM LETTER SEIZED AND UNMAILED
    Why is that other reseacher re-analyzing my data? What could possibly be the SRF's motivation here? Am I being phased out? What about the others? Please let me know immediately. It would be safer if you used my cover 14B file.

5
NOTES AND MANIFESTO
    Renegade SRF reporter found with unprocessed data on this vital subject. Although the reporter disappeared, the SRF found the following analysis, correlating to similar analyses found throughout the organization.

Manifesto Excerpts:
1. Group consciousness and individuality are the present issues.
2. We feel that the SRF group consciousness with its hierarchical structures and overt brain-washing techniques of reporter training deny the individual.
3. Despite emphasis on subjective data analysis, SRF attitude is officially intended to take certain thoughts and introduce them to mainstream culture.
4. When we approached headquarters with our findings, these were suppressed, and we were sent on missions which left little or no time to contemplate these ideas.
5. As the SRF perpetuates the present global pattern and only introduces "individuality" sparingly and always with the idea of dream manipulation or hier-

archical aristocracy which is information-based, we combined researchers, reporters, secretarial and data staff assert a registered complaint, with the desire that, aside from formal apology, the SRF release heretofore suppressed data and analyses concerning individuality.

6. If these criteria are not met, we will disperse and work as artists in society at large, individually introducing subjective versions of this understanding.

7. Without the cohesive structure of the SRF, but as vibrant personalities, the renegade SRF members will overtake the mainstream and will foster independent dreaming and future recognition.

8. This systematic inner dismantlement of SRF programs using its own methods will not be stoppable.

9. We therefore recommend that the SRF will take the action suggested above and release the information required.

Attached to the Manifesto excerpt was found this commentary from a high senior researcher:

Dear S___;

It saddens me greatly, as it must you, to send you this premature note which indicates all too well the very situation which we have worked to avoid. I definitely feel it is too soon for this action, and prematurely performed it will lead to the opposite of its intention. All indicators point to this, as we discussed last meeting. I reiterate that such impatient insertion of the ideas we have so carefully raised and fostered will only give the opposition carte blanche to destroy our work. I welcome your commentary, and remain your devoted student, H_____.

6

NOTES AND FRAGMENTS

Data gathered during hill tribe report appears relevant here. The battle between individuality and group consciousness is out in the open now. It is interesting to note that to defend the individual, the renegades formed an organization with a common goal.

***

An older retired researcher commented:

The idea that social research can be done on an individual basis is absurd. If these renegades were to look deeply into the question, they would realize how impossible such goals would be. Social research is just that, it is social. As such, individuals must continuously be in contact with and in shared consciousness with those who are subject/objects of study.

***

Another older researcher, ostensibly retired, but still very active in delicate fieldwork, emphasized again and again the clarity of pure research and continued support for the intention of the SRF, deploring the behavior which seems to

occur on all levels these days. "Predictions have indicated just exactly this fragmentation, and it is up to us to give an example, don't you think?" she said
recently. "I really believe that the SRF will triumph but one curious thing does
bother me. It has to do with a feeling. Well, how to say it? It is like a feeling way
at back that there is something not quite right, if you know what I mean. And
that has always been there, at back, since the beginning. I'm not the only one
to notice it, of course, it is definitely there. I feel that somehow this is at back
of all the troubles we are having now. Somehow if that were corrected - but first
it would have to be identified - then everything would run smooth again. I'm
certain of that." When asked if she had discussed this problem with any other
senior researchers, she just gave an enigmatic smile. "But dear, that's hardly the
point, is it?" she replied.

Translator's note: The data gathered concerning the renegades seems raw and
unanalyzed, simply assembled for the convenience of those whose concern it
was. Interestingly, it shows a number of definite viewpoints. Just who arranged
it is unclear, and the major data - The Individual File - was barely compiled,
consisting of marginal notes and riddle-like codes. Parts of the printout had been
torn off. What follows is what was left of The Individual File, with no attempt at
reconstruction by translators.

7
THE INDIVIDUAL FILE
-confidential
-private
-for separate viewing only

this is the only one - there is no other file - the individual unseparate yet is separate - personality expresses the individual
Advice: Keep the information to yourself. Know yourself. Express individuality
through research. Do not expect others to understand you. Do not look for ap-
proval, acceptance, group consciousness, family, friends, love, outside of your
own inner being. Balance all forces and formulae.
An individual is a person. Because an individual is neither an individual nor not
an individual, he is called an individual.
Handwritten notes: This data is too simple, it is not making sense. If the SRF
indeed has suppressed this data it must be in a code of some sort even now. In
the field we found far greater unfoldment of such ideas even prior to compilation. Something is wrong with this readout. It is too simple, it is too unclear.
What do you make of this?
I agree. I feel the file must be accessed differently. Perhaps this print data ac-
companies some symbolic visual or aural expression which contains the true
information?

8

THE TRUE

"All information concerning individuality and group consciousness which has previously been in circulation, either in mainstream or internally in the SRF, has been concealing vital aspects of the data analysis."

This statement was put out on a pamphlet and distributed through the SRF worldwide. Those responsible were called "renegades" by others but to themselves they were referred to as "the true". "The true" signed all such pamphlets and circulars with the words: THIS IS TRUE.

9

OFFICIAL REPORT

Until now, the SRF has been able to adjust to include all change, all dissent, all expansion and transformation. However, this split is by far the most difficult. Founding researchers are heartsore at the obstinacy of those proposing individuality without group consciousness. These dissidents are outraged by the established SRF view that group consciousness is more preferable, until preparation for individuality is completed. "All for one and one for all" has been forgotten and replaced by the simple cry, "me", or in some cases, "us". The division, despite all the insistence on art, on personality, on the artist as individual, occurs due to misunderstanding.

Compassionate senior researchers, 5 in number, with diverse special interests and particular arts and areas of research, meet regularly to attempt to modify both sides of the issue. The intense stream of input they analyze moment to moment does adjust and modify the situation somewhat and may in time bring about a new solution.

These 5 now meet under extraordinary circumstances in which they purposefully leave off their specific areas of interest, closing off much of the external data flow. In meeting one another on neutral ground they appear to absorb from one another essential shared data which later, when the meeting is over, seems to shed light on the situation. None can or will comment on these secret meetings.

Since these 5 gathered thus, the tension in the SRF has not held such a charge and in fact the work of the SRF continued even as it did before.

The researchers who were involved in the cry for individuality have formed a specific task force within the SRF for just such development. A few of the original instigators broke off to become artists, but interestingly, they report back often.

"It is the dawning of the new era, I am convinced," commented one senior researcher back at headquarters. "We really need them to be as far out there as humanly possible. And if they think they are individuals, so much the better for us all, for so they shall become."

10

COMMENTARY FOUND LATER CONCERNING THE INDIVIDUAL
FILE

I am convinced that this file was placed in the SRF enigmatically in
an encoded form. The question is, why? It seems to be reporting on internal
dynamics rather than "a group of individuals who hold certain beliefs" for example.

Those drawn to discover the file must break with all previous SRF
training, becoming, as it were, individuals in relation to other SRF workers. Yet
the file appears to lead nowhere.

Once the file is found and scanned, it is clearly only a hoax or riddle.
Images onscreen (not found in the printout but accessed by code B) include
sphinx, the back of a figure, a frieze of masked robed dancers animated in 3 or 4
jerky arm movements. Manipulation of the coding on a program level reveals a
few glyphs (unreadable) and nothing else.

Those who are pressing for release of this file will be very disappointed
that it does not hold more. After risking their positions in a prestigious research
foundation, risking even the destruction of the SRF itself due to internal strife,
they come only to a few words which make no sense, some images, and behind
it all, a few enigmatic indecipherable glyphs.

I suggest tactful withdrawal from this pursuit.

11

MARGINAL NOTE

This researcher failed to note that the glyphs are correspondent with
those found on an ancient ritual jade knife, now held in the Museum of Historical Anthropology. At first believed to be Chinese, it has been traced instead to
Aztec origin and usage, the Jade perhaps being traded. This ritual dagger is arrow
shaped and elaborately carved with scenery and glyphs. It was worn in ritual
costume.

A museum reconstruction of an ancient codex using models and di-
orama shows a priest figure wearing the carved jade arrow, drinking from an
elaborate ceremonial bowl offered by a priestess. A semicircle of women faces
the table at which the two share the ritual feast. On the table are reconstructions
of objects found in archeological digs, arranged according to a codex found near
the site. The objects include 5 painted terracotta images of women in dance
gesture with carved crystal indicators placed before each of them. The indicators also use this system of glyphs. A group of men cluster in the background
opposite to the semicircle of women - the men hold animals (for sacrifice?). The
women hold babies and offer loaves. The priest and priestess face the women.
One loaf is in the central position on the table, with painted terracotta "corn"
beside it.

Another reconstruction shows the priestess giving birth in squatting position while the priest offers in his hands the jade arrow to the emerging infant. They are surrounded by flowers. Behind the flowers is the semicircle of women, some holding loaves above their heads, others the painted terracotta corn.

One terracotta figurine shows a woman standing with a sheaf of wheat in her arms, as if it were an infant.

TRANSLATOR'S EPILOGUE

It is evident that the SRF data collected in the Laborer File is incomplete. Yet it does convey an accurate rendering of the view of the future given most credence during the mid-1980's.

It is, for the most part, true. The SRF research and analysis did reveal and create a great portion of future experience which we now take for granted. In this way, SRF findings did become common knowledge.

Despite the finger the SRF had placed on the pulse of the times, unexpected phenomena set back the work and only now are we beginning to pay homage to the pioneering work begun by that organization.

Had researchers then realized the value of their work to us today, they would surely have preserved even more of their data and analyses in print form, archaic as it may seem.

Translators are presently working on decoding other research data, and forthcoming volumes will cover topics as varied as Law, Surveillance, Linguistic Battles, Art and Code Analysis. These studies will be of vital interest to all historians of the 20th century.

The purpose of publication of these found documents lies in the meaning which can now be given to the work of the SRF. The few fragments we have been able to retreive shed light on our present times. It is as if a voice (or many voices) from the past were warning us against taking the wrong course of action.

How often have we presumed that the scholars of the past were unable to think as we do? Yet surely reading this document proves that, with allowance for facts about time and space which had not yet been revealed, the thought is as fresh and applicable now as then.

Of course, this is one star in a constellation of materials preserved from the 20th century. What continues to fascinate us, however, is the immediacy, the current which is unmistakable to us as "our present way of looking at things".

How often have we faced the same situations in organization, especially concerning reconstruction? Admittedly, with the new standards now in operation, we are in a very different field from the SRF. Our clarity over individuality and group consciousness, for example, seems to have evolved out of the early SRF explorations.

RITUAL REPORTS

Many of our seers attest to sensing SRF ritual reports, but found them incomprehensible. For example, "It was like a long dark room, with some kind of singing. Then 5 stood up wearing special colors, and one in white directed them in a dance. It was very different from our ceremonies, for nothing was sacrificed and the golden disc was not used. Then the crowd began a dance and ululation which was completely strange to me. It was gentle, not wild or savage as some have reported. No. I don't remember the words, but they moved their hands and arms in special ways which I do remember and have tried myself at home. They were thrown into an ecstasy or some kind of beautiful trance, and transmitted and received tremendous amounts of information, all of which was without meaning to me. It was beautiful but I couldn't understand it at all."

We have yet to decode this influx. Some of us did try using these fragments with the psychics to "recreate" the SRF ritual for exploratory purposes. To their amazement, they found themselves transported simultaneously into both the past and the future, and yet could not or would not articulate the basic decodation of that ritual. Saying they need to study it further, they have taken to performing this ritual on a monthly basis, calling it "an ancient dance ritual performance". It is very popular with young people in the cities.

TRANSLATION

Perhaps the translation of these SRF documents will help open up more of this fascinating bygone world, so it can merge with ours. Since the reconstruction, we have endeavoured in every way to bring into full being the ambitions and desires of humanity which were so thwarted during the tragic wars. Our simple way of life, much like the SRF description of the "electronic cottage" is based on principles of love, harmony and beauty.

Naturally there was a strong common unity among us, with the emphasis on art, which the SRF predicted. Our recovery and the retrieval of former wisdom has introduced some complications into our present world: we are more aware of the multiplicity of social forms coexisting, and of their almost clannish refusal to cooperate, except by official injunction (mostly ignored whenever possible).

These SRF materials, coming as they do at this time, offer interesting light. Some are reciting them in their original language, others have prepared visual versions.

The official translation committee feels that the documents, being on paper, should be republished on paper and offers this edition as the official edition.

Whenever possible, the translation committee has kept to the vernacular non-scientific translation. The entire untranslated record is held as museum data in the Central Clearing House Public Data Field.

7
GLOSSARY OF TERMS

Appropriate information: marketable information

Attractive Packaging: The presentation of information in such a way as to make it more marketable.

Audience: The buying public. (as in "Audience creation")

Biological solitude: a false concept of separated individuality which is currently common knowledge. This concept is often confused with the idea of an individual person or developed personality. However, the developed personality is not fooled by the idea of biological solitude.

Bureaucratic alchemy: As in the ancient alchemy: the turning of lead into gold; in this care, the use of elements of the current all-pervasive bureaucracy to reveal a hidden purity. Those involved in bureaucratic alchemy do not discover "gold" but become it.

Characterization of Persona Package: Also known as CPP. Usually chosen by researchers and reporters, according to criteria such as "attractive" and "appropriate", the CPP is a simulated personality or complete and well-acted persona, which includes clothing, movements, speech and thought patterns, ways of relating to others, objects and circumstances as well as interests and hobbies. The CPP is in place at all times and will even enhance and direct dreams. A polished CPP is essential to all researchers, and the ability to shift CPP when necessary is also a respected skill. The CPP may or may not resemble PI (Personal Identity). The CPP can also be known as "cover".

Common Knowledge: Those ideas which have penetrated the thought of the general populace and of which everyone has heard are referred to as common knowledge. It could be said to be the external version of the dream equasion. Some examples of common knowledge which have recently come to be known are UFO's, nuclear war, individual freedom, public health care and education. Opinions on common knowledge vary, but the awareness of the ideas is what is specific to common knowledge. Like the unicorns of medieval times, that which is common knowledge need not be a physical reality, nor need it be thought of by everyone as good or even real, but the idea circulating is enough to give it status. The electronic cottage, for example, is becoming common knowledge.

Documentary Print: Direct and time-related reportage in print form, more re-lated to the film and video descriptor "documentary" than to the earlier use of documentary which involves documents. In the old sense of documentary, docu-mentary print seems redundant, but in a visual and audio world, documentary print takes the film and video awareness and retranslates it back to words again.

Dream Equation: This term refers to the status quo as it is held in the unseen dream and archetype thought imagery of a society. It is a balancing of dream im-agery which has power to influence the actions, decisions, and sensibilities of a people. A change in the dream equation changes the social balance. Equillibrium is restored by a new dream equation.

Electronic Cottage (ElCott): The homeplace/workplace which becomes more prominent in society as information becomes the main commodity of the mar-ketplace. The term is not new, and is in fact an idea which is common knowl-edge.

Extended Enhancement: The first stage of change and evolution of group con-sciousness, as experienced from the point of view of change from biological soli-tude.

Fixation: An imbalance of mind in a researcher, during which information circu-lation is stopped or blocked, ecologically affecting the entire being.

Fresh Mind (FM): Direct Perception

Fresh Mind Exhaustion: Use of concepts, indirect perception

Future Phases (esp. Phase I, Phase II): The SRF has grouped experiences of the future into various phases roughly categorized as Phase I, Phase II, etc. These future phases are experienced subjectively by researchers and reported back to headquarters where the information is introduced to the general public by vari-ous means. In this way, the future becomes common knowledge before it actu-ally "hits the streets". The future phases are categorized according to SRF criteria from an amalgamation of reports, with the average stages being identified by cross-referencing innumerable individual screenings.

Group Consciousness: Awareness of extended enhancement, or the realization of more than biological solitude. It can occur between two people as love or friendship, between families and groups of friends, communities, or nations, or humanity or all of life, or all that is, was and will be. It is not clearly understood but researchers in future phases agree that consciousness of more than biological solitude is common knowledge even in the pre-research past, which indicates that "there is nothing new under the sun".

Implicate: To explain or display ideas or features by indirect means.

Indians of Luxury: Those living in the future, particularly those who are indigenous to the future living now within the present.

Information Circulation: An ecological situation, in which the Fresh MInd is present in a researcher, allowing the free flow of sense and ideation data without fixation or stoppage.

Infrastructure: All carriers of information, their linkages, their pathways and methods.

Intensified Personalization: This is a negative state which spells danger to all researchers. It involves "taking things personally" and implies lack of Pattern Guard, a fault in the CPP, and renders the research useless.

Key Personalities: Those whose CPP is used as part of the infrastructure for the relay of information, particularly through media.

Lab of Luxury: The area of interest of the researcher, which includes the inner and outer being of the researcher, and the ecological balance of the dream equation, the media environment, the urban or rural physical environment.

Lay-Viewer: One interested in research who has not trained nor been involved in any public disclosure.

Link-Launch: An experiment in which many researchers were catapulted into a variety of fields simultaneously, with the instructions to report back within a specific time period. It was an interesting experiment, but results showed that maturity of researchers is imperative in the success of further link-launch activities.

Luxury: The present condition, in which all manner of goods and services are available for the majority of users, none of whom have to make these items for themselves.

Most Observable Information (MOI): The use of Fresh Mind produces the Most Observable Information (MOI) which is an accurate scan of any situation, real or mediated. The first step to subjective valuation of information.

Multiple-Matrix (as in MM researcher): Refers to involvement in a variety of future phases or a variety of social/emotional/political fields simultaneously, with ease of transport from one to the other.

Pattern Guard: An inner program which ensures that the situation is kept intact and does not revert to chaos, wind down to entropy, or explode under pressure. Used extensively by researchers, particularly in difficult situations, the Pattern Guard keeps CPP in place. Some example types of Pattern Guard are "moral duty" and "experiment view". The Pattern Guard is uniquely tailored to each individual researcher, permanently implanted with a range of modulations suited to preserving the chosen CPP.

Personal Criteria: All information in the SRF is sorted according to the personal criteria of the researchers involved. This is not codified, nor is it influenced by the CPP. Fresh Mind is really of benefit in the development of Personal Criteria.

Personal Identity: Also known as PI, this is a phase of understanding previous to the CPP, and most lay-people now are not interested in the development of PI, only of a successful CPP which is much more marketable. Charming as PI may be, it is subject to problems. For one thing, those with PI are now a minority, and often do not speak the same language (of movement, clothing, speech style, dream type) as the majority which uses an easily translatable CPP. Unlike researchers, the generality is limited by the CPP and cannot change at will, having almost entirely identified with it as self, thereby confusing PI with CPP completely. In most cases, except in the charming naives which sometimes unwittingly become media prominent for a short time only, the PI is a detriment to success in a high speed world. The SRF is introducing this concept as common knowledge soon.

Phase Shift: The marked change from one future phase to another has been referred to as a phase shift. For example, the shift usually involves a need to report as quickly as possible. It also may include a complete change of interest or attitude.

Reportage: The activity of relaying information.

Reporter: One who relays information.

Researcher: May also be a reporter, but one who is trained to explore and reveal within and beyond the dream equation.

Ritual: The use of patterns to transpose realities.

Scan: Now that reading is heavily influenced by visual and audio orientations, it is referred to as scanning, and in "scanning the screen".

Typical: That CPP which contains as many similar points of contact with as many other CPPs as possible is referred to as "typical".

View: To scan or read, to accept visual information.

Viewer: The one who scans or reads; also, the general public, audience or market.

Voluntary Implicity: Voluntary entry into the field of that which is implied in that which is viewed or heard, to foster a greater understanding.

White Paper: A believable official presentation of print material.

World Being: A representative of the tribe who manipulates symbols in present time.

Worthless: Not marketable.

8
APPENDIX

APHORISMS AND SLOGANS

• Nothing is new under the sun.
• Common knowledge has become a manipulatable commodity in the information warehouse.
• Personalized sorting generates meaning from information.
• All statements subject to revision.
• Realtime is our watchword at the SRF.
• Subjectivity creates high grade information.
• The only cure for research stress is reportage.
• Thank heavens for Fresh Mind!
• Although all data is personalized, don't take it personally!
• The SRF is willing to change.
• What is relevant data?
• The techs are in check when art is in the picture.
• A good spy lives his cover.
• Documentary print speaks authoritatively and appears to be true.
• Art is the answer.
• Stating the obvious requires specialized language if that information is to be profitably marketed.

APPENDIX II

ALTERNATE PRESENTATION MODES
The Research Context Committee eventually chose Context IV (Social Science Fiction) as the appropriate presentation mode for this material. Other contexts were under consideration but were found to be unsuitable for SRF purposes. The contexts considered were:
I. The Factual Report
II. New Journalism
III. Incendiary Internal Documents
IV. Social Science Fiction
V. Choose Your Own Context

NOTES FOR THE SRF DOCUMENT FRAMES
(TAKEN FROM RESEARCH CONTEXT COMMITTEE DATA):

I. The Factual Report
The attitude is straightforward. The pages are as they are. The introduction simply expresses that they are released documents from the SRF spanning the years 1983-1985. Little or no explanation is required, as from this point of view, the work speaks for itself.

II. New Journalism
The introduction would define this journalistic technique. What is actually being represented in these pages, from this viewpoint, is internal mappings and minimalist notations of emotional waves, presented in an art form using documentary print as the medium. The work is more internally-referencing than most New Journalism, but the intent is to establish this internal-referencing as valid journalistic material. Each section is a new personality phase, and the monitoring by direct documentation gives an accurate rendering of varied emotional states, all set in a writing style using a variety of sets and viewpoints to express these emotional phases. In every part, the subjective attitude is never lost, although it may be masked.

III. Incendiary Internal Documents
This is a complex framing method which appeals to the sense of intrigue in the reader. These documents are seen as internally circulated among members of the SRF, organized during the mid-80's. The internal circulation of these ideas is intended to be inflammatory, and to bring about radical changes in the organization. The edition printed here does exclude sections in which names are named and fault is found with specific individuals. The work appears to be partly fictional / partly true, and is intended to cause widespread dissent which will

lead to eventual transformation of the SRF. Many of the sections on problems, etc. seem to be fictionalized versions of actual bureaucratic episodes within the organization. Other parts are included to point out faults or to specifically perpetrate the views of those circulating the document. It is read only within the SRF, where it causes great damage in the form of anger, scandal and general mistrust and unrest. On the positive side, there is a purification of the organization intended by the so-called troublemakers which makes its work in the end more brilliant and with much greater circulation of life-force, room for new ideas. The document is seen as being circulated within the activist group in this first draft form before being released publicly.

IV. Social Science Fiction

Here we have a large capacity which will be termed Social Science Fiction. In Canada we have little science fiction, and what there is has been written from a view to technology. Although this book springs from technology in "the wired future", it examines social issues, almost in as boring a manner as Canadian high school social studies. The leap into Social Science Fiction occurs in the framing method, which is delineated in the introduction, translator's notes and throughout the text.

V. Choose Your Own Context

The final frame offered to the reader is one of assimilating and synthesizing the different elements as displayed here, choosing any, all or none of the above frames. The book then becomes an interactive document. Choose Your Own Context, or U-Frame-It, involves the reader directly.

How it works: The contexts are coded I, II, III, IV. The reader chooses the path by which the book is to be read by choosing one of the context codes. These codes are footnoted throughout the text, indicating where and how to read next. The notes and indicators draw the reader along the chosen path according to the context chosen. There are, then, four different versions of the book being held within one seemingly cohesive document. There could be four different versions or viewpoints at any one time, and this does not include the comprehensive view of the whole, which stands as another version also.

Although this context was chosen by the Research Context Committee as the best and most accurate, it was eventually rejected in this public version in order that the document be more approachable and more easily marketed.

The Most Marketable context was considered to be Social Science Fiction, and it was even deliberated that a plot line could be introduced to make the information more attractive. At the time of this writing, the Research Context Committee is disbanding, with the Edit/Format Group taking on the remainder of the presentational responsibilities.

END OF DOCUMENT

About This Book

I wrote this book episodically and by hand in the early 1980's, before the personal computer, well before the internet's world wide web, and long before blogs. It was intended to be a real-time document of interior processes, with a few excursions into description of exterior events. I didn't edit it for this edition, but publish it here as it was originally written.

What I've found over the years is that this odd document has proven to be somewhat prophetic, both personally and sociologically. For example, in the 1990's I met and later married that artist the researcher had seen and described in the Researcher's Diary! Not to mention the rise of individual and public reporting on an unimagined scale via the blogging community. Maybe researchers did enter the future!

It was those resonances, combined with my desire to share this writing, that encouraged me to publish this again. In 1985 I self-published a photocopied version with hand-stitched binding, but, like the SRF documents described in the book, the few I had left were stored for years in containers, unseen.

I'm not sure if there actually is a real-world Social Research Foundation, so hope there is no copyright infringement here. I am aware now that the initials SRF are also used as shorthand for the Yogananda group, Self Realization Fellowship. Similarly, the initials CPP (which I use here to indicate Characterization of Persona Package) are also used in Canada by the government to mean Canada Pension Plan.

I was writing this at a cusp of societal change, when the introduction of the computer society was about to enter the personal realm, radically reorganizing everyone's way of life. I see it as a cry of the heart as it is being submerged by the analytical and ultimately bureaucratic forces of that coming new era.

- Carol Sill

www.ingramcontent.com/pod-product-compliance
Lightning Source LLC
Chambersburg PA
CBHW031217270326
41931CB00006B/594